WITHDRAWN

C333706634

PHOTO ART

35 ways to use old and new photographs

Ellie Laycock

CICO BOOKS
LONDON NEW YORK

This book is dedicated to my wonderful friend Claire Richardson, who took me under her wing and showed me how to blossom. Your love and light deeply touched many of us all around the world. Until we meet again, my sister.

Published in 2015 by CICO Books
An imprint of Ryland Peters & Small Ltd

20–21 Jockey's Fields   341 E 116th St
London WC1R 4BW   New York, NY 10029
www.rylandpeters.com

10 9 8 7 6 5 4 3 2 1

A CIP catalog record for this book is available from the Library of Congress and the British Library.

ISBN: 978-1-78249-191-0

Printed in China

Editor: Sarah Hoggett
Designer: Vicky Rankin
Illustrator: Harriet de Winton
Photographer: James Gardiner
Stylist: Joanna Thornhill
Templates: Stephen Dew

Editor: Carmel Edmonds
In-house designer: Fahema Khanam
Art director: Sally Powell
Production manager: Gordana Simakovic
Publishing manager: Penny Craig
Publisher: Cindy Richards

CONTENTS

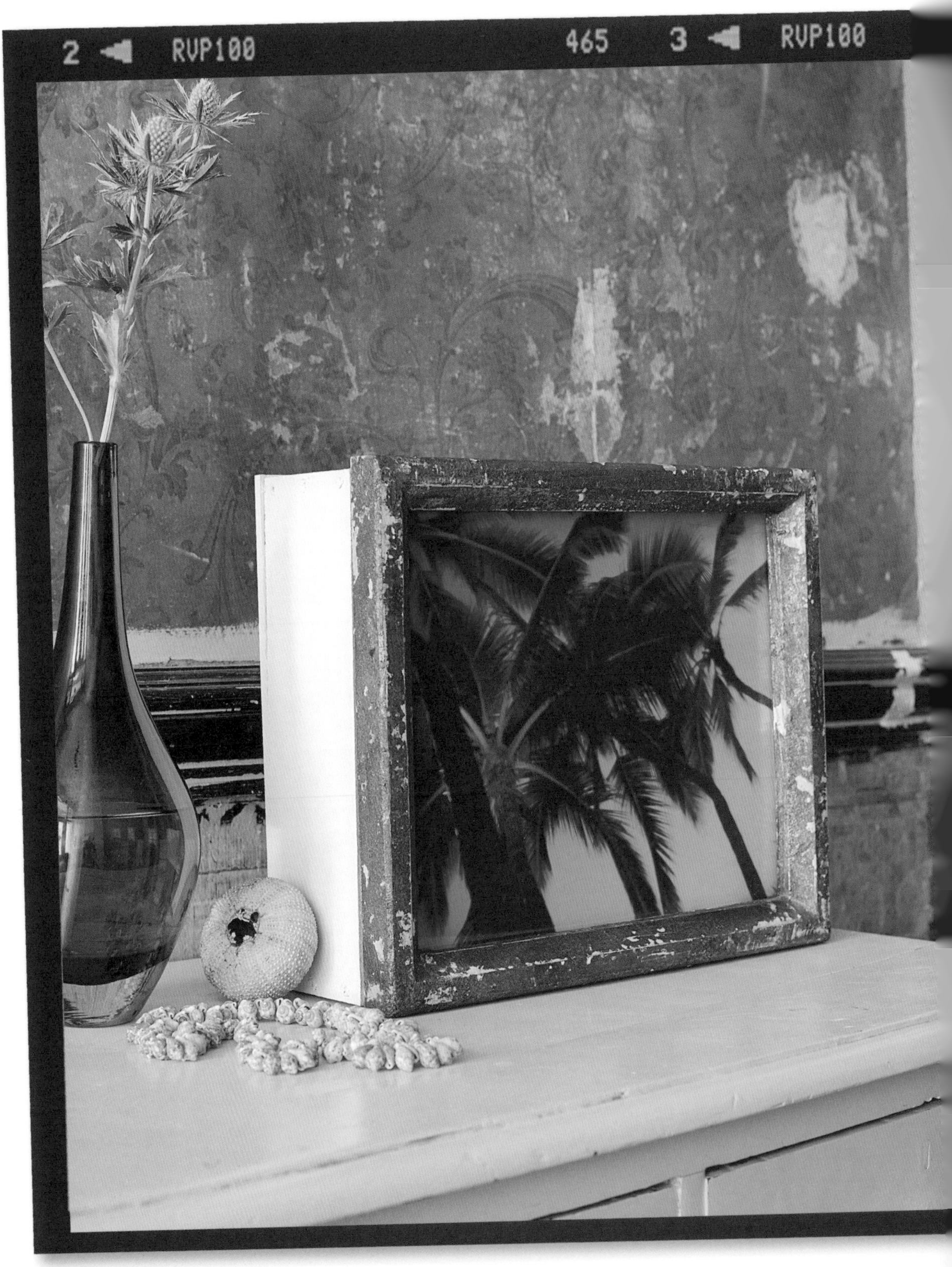
2 RVP100
465
3 RVP100

INTRODUCTION

I love old photographs. In fact, it doesn't even matter if I don't know the people or places in them. Many people are now gone or grown up, the holiday's a memory—those photos capture a moment in time. I guess I'm just nostalgic.

But it set me thinking: how many of us have half-remembered photos hidden away in dusty albums or boxes that rarely get opened, tucked up in paper packets from the lab, languishing lost on hard drives or in virtual camera rolls that vanish on an empty battery? Too precious to throw away—and yet we never quite get round to framing them. What if we could do something amazing and new with them? Bring them to life again? Celebrate them for the special things that they are?

This book is designed to do just that and features a wide range of creative projects—from decorating furniture for the home to making personalized gifts for others—using all of the different types of photograph that you may have, both analog and digital.

As for subject matter, most subjects will work with most of these projects. Left to my own devices, I'd probably create every project with lovely vintage photos of people past. To avoid that, and to show you how interchangeable it all is, I've used a variety of color and black-and-white images, from old and analog to new, digital, app-driven, or social media-sourced imagery. The photos showcase people, places, holidays, births, marriages, special locations or scenes, favorite meals, cars, and pets—in short, the type of photos that we all take and that mean something to us. Feel free to swap your own images into any of the projects. In fact, I encourage you to. At least try it—you may just create something wonderful!

Ellie Laycock

WORKING WITH PHOTOGRAPHS

In this section you'll discover some of the basic techniques you'll need for the projects, including advice on copying your paper prints and easy ways to manipulate digital images.

MAKING COPIES OF ORIGINAL PHOTOGRAPHS

I advocate using copies of original photos whenever possible for all of the projects in this book. I'd hate for anyone to lose a precious photo via an unfortunate accident with some glue or scissors. There are three ways to create a copy of an original photo suggested here.

Scanning

If you have a scanner (or a combined printer/scanner) at home, then this is the easiest way to digitize a paper print (film scanners are also available for scanning transparencies or negatives). All scanners vary, but the process will be something like this:

1 Make sure the scanner is connected to the computer and powered up.

2 Navigate to the scanning software on your computer and open it by double clicking or pressing the "scan" button on your scanner.

3 Open the scanner lid and check that it is clean and free of dust.

4 Place the photograph, also free from dust, image side down in the center of the glass surface of the scanner and close the lid.

5 Select your scanning preferences. Here you can select to scan in black and white or in color, the resolution (300 dpi is optimal) and the format (JPEG is recommended). Other options can include where to save your scan, the name of the scan, the size etc.

6 Select "Preview" to check your settings.

7 Click "Scan" or "Finish" to scan the image. (If you have any trouble, try using the Scan Wizard or other inbuilt help program to guide you.)

8 Finish by saving the image onto your computer.

Digital reproduction

Use a digital camera or smart phone to take a digital picture of your original photograph.

1 Lay the original down flat in an area lit evenly by natural light (cloudy days are best—direct sunlight is too harsh and artificial light gives a yellow color cast).

2 Hold the camera directly above the original image—as flat on as possible, but pulled back enough to ensure the original is fully visible in the viewfinder—and take several shots.

3 Plug the camera into your computer and download the shots. If you're using a smartphone, you can use a streaming service like My Photo Stream or even email the photo to yourself from the smartphone, then open the email on your computer and download the photo from there.

Photocopying

Take your original photographs to a copyshop, where you can have them copied in color or black and white. They should also be able to reproduce your photographs in a mirror image (useful for image transfer techniques), darken or lighten them, or enlarge or reduce the sizes.

CREATING A WHITE BACKGROUND ("CUTTING OUT")

This is not a computer manipulation, but a simple way of creating a white background for your subject. Print out the complete image onto photo paper and let it dry. Cut around your subject with scissors, then stick your subject down on a fresh piece of white office paper. Scan this back into your computer (or if you don't have a scanner, take a digital photo of it laid flat instead): now your subject has been "cut out"!

BASIC DIGITAL EDITS

Most computer systems come with some form of basic image-editing software, but if yours doesn't, there are free online versions available—see Useful Resources on pages 142-3.

The following instructions are based on using PicMonkey, but can be applied to other programs.

Uploading your photo

Click on "Edit", then click on the computer symbol to open the browser window. Navigate to your desired photo, click on the file, then click the "Open" box at the bottom right of the window.

Crop

Use the crop tool to get rid of unwanted edges. Click and drag the tops or sides to move the selection area or the corners to move both sides simultaneously. Click "Apply" to finish.

Rotate

This tool allows you to rotate your image clockwise or anticlockwise, flip it horizontally (useful for image transfer techniques) or vertically, or to straighten up the image. Click "Apply" when done.

Exposure

Here you can adjust the brightness to make your photo lighter or darker overall, the highlights to make the lightest tones of your photo lighter still, the shadows to darken the shadows, and the contrast, which increases or decreases contrast by affecting the highlights and the shadows at the same time. High contrast is when the shadows are very black and the highlights are very white; low contrast is when the photo looks quite gray and dull overall.

Try the "Auto Adjust" button if you want the software to decide for you.

Sharpen

Slide the sharpness slider to the right if you need to sharpen your photograph (make it less blurred).

Colors

If the photo has a color cast or looks a bit odd, select "Neutral Picker" and then click on a white or gray area of the photo to bring the color balance back to normal. Slide the "Saturation" bar to the right to make the colors more saturated or to the left to desaturate the image; all the way to the left will give you a black-and-white image. The "Temperature" slider adjusts the amount of blue and yellow in the photo—as a rule, cameras see daylight as blue and artificial light as yellow, so if your indoor photo is yellow, try sliding the slider toward blue to correct it. Alternatively, try the "Auto Adjust" button.

Making a negative

Create a negative from a digital photo by selecting "Image" followed by "Adjustment," then "Invert." To make it black and white, you can either select "Image," then "Mode," and select "Grayscale," or to have more control over the conversion, you can instead select "Image," "Adjustments," then "Black and White."

Resize

To scale an image, use the "Resize" tool. Life would be easier if we could enter a measurement here in inches or centimetres (and in some software you can, so use that if at all possible), but most online editors want to know how many pixels you need. The reason for this, without going too far into it, is that a digital photo is made up of lots of pixels (tiny squares of color) and if it's going to be printed, then the final size of the print depends on what resolution it is printed at. Resolution is measured in pixels per inch (PPI*) and the closer the pixels are together when printed, the smaller the print size will be.

So let's select 300 PPI as our default resolution (a nice high-quality photo setting). That means a photo of 300 x 300 pixels will print at 1 x 1 in. (2.5 x 2.5 cm), 600 x 600 pixels at 2 x 2 in. (5 x 5 cm), and so on. To find the value for a 10-in. (25-cm) tall photo, multiply 10 (inches) x 300 (pixels) (=3000) and enter that value into the height box.

Tick the "Keep Proportions" box if you want your image to scale up in ratio, otherwise the photo will become distorted. You only need to enter one size value into one of the boxes and the other will be calculated automatically.

Click "Apply" when done.

(For an alternative method of scaling up an image to a standard paper size, please see "Scale to Fit Media" on page 15.)

*PPI and DPI (dots per inch) are interchangeable for the purposes of this text.

Effects (Magic Wand symbol)

In here are lots of toys to play with if you want to take your photos further.

Note the "Tint" tool, which can be used for the Statement Photo Drawers project on page 104. Under "Color," move the little white circle until it is over the desired color. Near the top is more muted color and near the bottom is intense, very saturated color. The "Fade" slider below fades the color in and out over your photo. Click "Apply" when done.

The "Black and White" and "Sepia" tools can be used for converting color photos to non color, while the "Dodge" and "Burn" brushes (found in the "Advanced" section) allow you to paint lighter or darker areas into your photos (as used in the Repurposed Vintage Paper Print project on page 80).

SAVING FILES

Click the "Save" button. You will be asked to give the file a name and select a file extension. Choose .jpg here (which saves your file in the JPEG format—the universal format for photos).

If possible, select the highest quality when saving. This preserves the most detail in the photo, but does mean larger file sizes on your system.

Click "Save to My Computer," where you should have another chance to rename the file (if required) and decide where to save this new file. Then click "Save." To avoid overwriting your previous edits, save each new version with a new filename.

PRINTING OUT YOUR COPIES

Both inkjet and laser printers are great for making copies, and laser prints can also be used for image transfer projects (see "Image transfer" on page 15).

There are many different brands of printers, each with their own unique interfaces, but here is a rough guide to the general features you may find.

Click on "File" and scroll down to "Print" to open the print dialog box where you will see these options:

Printer
Select which printer to use or add a new printer.

Copies
Input the number of prints you wish to make.

Paper size

Select the size of paper to print onto. There are defaults for standard-sized office paper and photo paper, or you can input custom-sized paper here (under "Manage Custom Sizes").

Orientation (or Page Setup)

Select portrait or landscape here.

Quality & media/Media type

Tell the printer what kind of paper you want to print on—glossy photo paper, plain office paper, clear acetate, and so on—then make sure you load the same paper, ensuring the size corresponds with the Paper Size (see left).

Quality & media/Paper source

This depends on your particular printer, but usually the paper will feed in from the "Rear Tray."

Quality & media/Print quality

Choose from "High" (for quality photos), "Standard," or "Fast" (which uses the least ink).

Grayscale printing

Check this box and the printer will print in black and white, even if you're sending a color image to print. If you are expecting color prints and they come out black and white, this is the first place to troubleshoot.

Mirror image printing

You can flip images (without needing editing software) using the printer's dialog box.

What you're looking for here is a box to tick called "Mirror Image" or "Mirror" or "Flip Horizontally." Look under "Layout," "Properties," or "Basics" tabs to find it. Click the "Print Preview" button first to see on screen what the printer intends to do before committing to printing (and wasting ink!).

Image transfer

Just a quick note on copies used in image transfer. As a rule, inkjet prints won't work. This is because they are printed in such a way that the ink soaks into the paper and will not release to make a transfer. Toner-based laser copies are printed with a powder-based toner that is heat sealed just onto the paper surface, and so can be released again either with heat or solvent. Some laser printers and copiers produce copies that work better than others, so experiment to find one that works for you.

"Scale to Fit Media" or "Scale to Fit Paper Size"

This little box is very important! If you have scaled your image in the software already, then do not check this box, because it will resize your image again to fit onto the selected paper media, undoing your hard work.

On the other hand, it can be a simple way to scale a photo up or down to fit onto the paper without needing editing software, so tick the box if that is what you require.

Chapter 1
Framing and Display

There's not much point in taking photos if they're permanently stored away in a box or on your computer—so why not display your favorites for all to see? The great news is that you can do far more than just put them in a pretty frame or album. This chapter sets out a whole host of imaginative ideas, from upcycled photo stands to put on your desk at work to mega-sized images that will form a focal point in any room. You can even find out how to incorporate photos into various pieces of furniture, creating statement pieces that will be the envy of all your friends.

FAMILY SNAPSHOT SHELVING

This sweet little house-shaped shelving unit was an eBay find, but you can use any type or size of shelving you like. Fill with your favorite family snapshots or create collages for larger recess spaces, and use as a photo display or quirky backdrop to your ornaments.

You will need

- Shelving unit or small bookcase
- Family snapshots
- Plain office paper (or glossy or matt photo paper, if you prefer)
- Repositionable spray adhesive
- Measuring tape or ruler
- Printer (or copies from copyshop)
- Scissors
- Craft knife

Optional

- Self-adhesive label paper for your printer
- Varnish
- Paintbrush

1 Measure the area you'd like to cover with photos. My "house" has various-sized recesses, so I measured each one and made a note of the dimensions.

2 Resize your photos to fit your measurements (see page 12). Print the photos onto your paper of choice—I used plain office paper with settings as follows: plain paper, medium print quality, grayscale—but you could use glossy or matt photo paper instead. You could even print onto self-adhesive label paper for laser or inkjet printers (see step 4). Alternatively, take your photos to a copy shop and get black-and-white laser copies or enlargements made. Then transfer your measurements onto your favorite parts of the photos and cut to size.

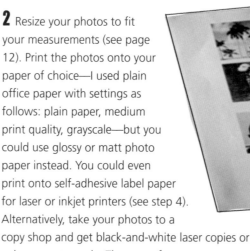

3 Cut out your photos. Check that they fit the recesses by dropping them in, trimming off any excess paper if necessary.

FURTHER IDEAS

- Use color for a bolder effect—select images that have the same colors, hues, and tones for a strong look.

- Use the photos to indicate what belongs in each recess. For example, a snapshot of your rosemary bush in the garden could be pasted behind the rosemary jar on the kitchen shelf.

- Create a small shelving unit that would be ideal for displaying mementos and trinkets by repurposing a wooden cutlery drawer, then adding photos to the recesses.

4 On a protected surface, spray adhesive onto the back of the first photo. Alternatively, if you used self-adhesive label paper in step 2, peel away the backing paper on the first image.

5 Carefully lift up the photo and start to position it in the chosen recess. Line up one edge first and then gently roll the rest of the image down flat. If it's not quite straight, use the blade of the craft knife to gently lift an edge up so that you can remove and reposition it. If you do find that there's any excess paper going over the edge, use the craft knife to trim it off.

6 Push down firmly. Repeat until all the photos are in position. Let dry. You could then seal the photos with varnish, if desired.

GO-LARGE PRINT

Have you got a favorite photo that you would like to see super-sized and turned into a striking wall display? Do it yourself with these simple steps to turn a snapshot into a piece of art. You decide the scale—no frame required.

You will need

- Digital photo or scan of analog image
- US letter size (A4) photo paper
- Repositionable spray adhesive
- US letter size (A4) pieces of foam board
- Inkjet or laser printer
- White cotton gloves
- Craft knife, metal rule, and cutting mat

Optional

- Adhesive pads or Blu-tack to attach boards to wall

1 Prepare your digital photograph for printing (see page 10). Use a high-resolution image for clarity; if you don't mind a pixelated or grainy effect, you can use a low-resolution image (see page 12).

2 Choose an online image-tiling site (see page 143) or use free software for iOS devices. Upload your image. Select how many "tiles" you would like and on what paper size. I chose US letter (A4) paper, landscape and three sheets wide, which resulted in a 3 x 3 grid (see tip box, right). See what works for you within the preview features. Save the results by downloading the tiles.

3 Print your tiles on your chosen paper. I like matte photo paper. Let dry.

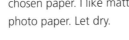

Tiling images

The tiling service takes your original photo and cuts it up based on what you've asked it to do. I asked for my image to be three US letter (A4) landscape sheets wide, so it calculated that the whole image would fit over three columns and four rows. The top three rows had each tile full of image, while the bottom row just had a small strip of image on each tile (because the ratio of the photo didn't exactly match the ratio of the paper laid out in a 3 x 3 grid). I didn't print these small strips because they were surplus to requirements, so the final image is slightly cropped at the base compared to the original photo.

4 On a protected work surface, apply spray adhesive to the back of the first tile and stick it onto a foam board. Wearing white cotton gloves to avoid marking your prints with fingerprints, smooth the tile down flat. You don't have to be exact as you will trim off the white borders anyway—just make sure that the printed part is all on the foam board. Let dry. Repeat with all the other tiles, keeping them in order.

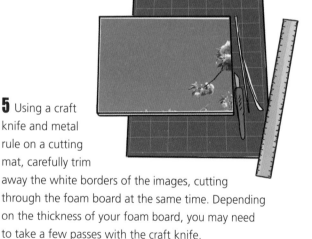

5 Using a craft knife and metal rule on a cutting mat, carefully trim away the white borders of the images, cutting through the foam board at the same time. Depending on the thickness of your foam board, you may need to take a few passes with the craft knife.

6 Add self-adhesive pads or Blu-tack to the backs of the foam boards and you're ready to fix them straight onto the wall!

FURTHER IDEAS

- Don't want to stick things on your wall? Use a single-hole punch to make a hole in each corner, then string the tiles together to create a "chainmail" poster. (Bath chain and connectors from a plumber's supply store make perfect adjustable loops!)

- Swap out some tiles for other images to create an abstract artwork.

- Cover a whole wall to create your own personalized wallpaper! Prepare the wall with lining paper first and leave out the foam-board steps.

- If you stick the photo prints to the foam boards accurately and do not cut away the white borders, it creates an interesting framed effect.

- Get creative with what you photograph. Take a shot of your child's funniest drawing, a close-up of a beautiful flower from your garden, or that view from your hotel balcony, and get super-sizing!

PANORAMIC BENCH

When I travel and find myself in new and amazing landscapes, my instinct is to document my environment in a panorama. I used to take lots of photos, pivoting on the spot and then sticking the prints together, but these days most digital cameras and smart phones have a "panorama" function. This project shows you how to create a personalized and bespoke panoramic bench out of these otherwise difficult-to-frame images.

You will need

- Bench
- Digital photo or scan of analog image
- Glossy photo paper
- PVA glue and water mix (two parts glue mixed with one part water) or Mod Podge
- Varnish
- Medium-grit sandpaper
- Damp cloth
- Tape measure
- Craft knife, metal rule, and cutting mat
- Foam brush
- Paintbrush
- Pin

Optional

- White cotton gloves
- Roller

1 Prepare your surface by lightly sanding the bench to create a key for your adhesive. Wipe with a damp cloth to remove any dust.

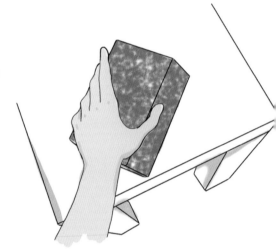

2 Measure the top of your bench. Then, using photo-editing software, prepare your panorama. Enlarge, crop, and/or scale your image (see pages 10 and 12) to the size of the bench. Now divide the image into equal sections that can be printed: for example, my bench was 35 in. (90 cm) and could therefore be divided into five sections, each 7 in. (18 cm) wide. Use the crop tool fixed at this size and save each section as a separate file to print.

3 Print your photo sections. Make sure that you have the "Scale to Fit Media" box unchecked in the printer dialog box, as you don't want the printer to adjust your print sizes. I printed the five sections on gloss photo paper on the high-quality print setting (see page 14). Allow the prints to dry. Alternatively, order a custom-sized print from one of the suppliers suggested on page 142.

4 Using a craft knife and a metal rule on a cutting mat, carefully trim off the white borders. You may wish to wear cotton gloves to protect the prints.

5 Apply a thin layer of the PVA glue and water mix or Mod Podge to the bench top, and smooth it out with a foam brush.

6 Lay out your sections in the correct order and begin applying them to the bench, working from one side to the other. You may wish to wear clean cotton gloves to avoid getting fingerprints on the images. Smooth out any wrinkles with gloved hands or a clean, dry roller.

7 Once the images are in place and have dried, paint a very thin layer of the PVA glue and water mix over the top to seal the ink. Let dry for an hour and smooth out any bubbles that appear. (Get rid of stubborn bubbles by pricking them with a pin and smoothing down.) Once the first coat has dried, apply a second thin coat.

8 Once completely dry and flat, seal with varnish.

Neat edges

To get the edges really flat, after pressing down, cover the bench with spare sheets of paper (to protect the prints) and then place heavy flat objects over the top to keep them flat until the glue is dry. Magazines or heavy books are good for this.

FURTHER IDEAS

- Rather than using one long image, create your own designs using a selection of photos, cut-outs, and even text to create a découpage or collage design.

- Add a drop of color—or even fine-grade glitter—to the varnish to create a tinted sealant for a different look.

CUSTOM MEMORY BOX

This project turns a plain cardboard box into a customized memory box to keep those treasured mementos safe— perfect as either a unique gift or a creative way of storing those cherished moments. For added versatility, this design allows you to change the photograph at will.

You will need

- Pre-made box (available from craft stores and stationers)
- Decorative photo frame
- Craft knife, long and short metal rules, and cutting mat
- Pencil
- All-purpose glue
- Old magazines (to apply pressure while glue dries)
- Photo to fit frame
- Photo paper
- Inkjet or laser printer

Optional

- Paint (watered-down chalk paint)
- Paintbrush
- Scissors
- Card stock (card) for replacement frame back

1 Measure the lid of the box. Select a photo frame that is smaller (or exactly the same size) as the lid. Remove the back panel of the frame, any paper inside, and the glass or Perspex, leaving you with just the frame.

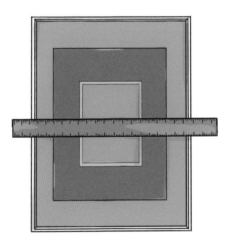

2 Place the lid right side down on your work surface. Center the frame (also right side down) inside the lid. Use a ruler to help you. Also measure from the inside edge of the frame aperture to just past any fixings that hold the back of the frame in the center—on my frame this was ¾ in. (2 cm)—and note this measurement for later.

3 Hold the frame in position and draw around the inside and outside edges in pencil. Then extend out from the inner rectangular line by the measurement taken in step 2 and mark this new line, again using a ruler and pencil. This will allow the fixings of the frame to be accessible for easy insertion of the photograph. Using a craft knife and metal rule on a cutting mat, carefully cut along the cut line and remove the central piece of the lid.

4 If required, paint the box lid and/or the box base to complement your chosen frame. Use a very light coat of paint and leave to dry, then repeat if needed (one thick coat of paint may damage the box, so test on the cut-away section of the lid first).

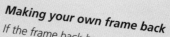

Making your own frame back

If the frame back has a stand attached that cannot be easily removed, cut your own replacement back out of card stock (card). If the frame is deep, insert several layers until the clasps hold the new back firmly in place.

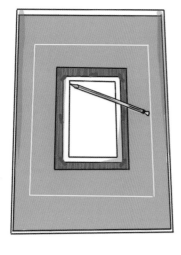

5 Place the frame face down on your work surface, with the lid face down centrally over the top. The fixings should be visible through the hole you've just cut. Using a pencil, draw on the back of the frame around the inside of the hole cut in the lid; you can follow this line when gluing the lid in place.

6 Set the lid aside. Apply all-purpose glue to the back of the frame in the areas between the outer edge of the frame and the pencil line you drew in the previous step. Now replace the lid and gently move it into position, following the pencil guidelines. Place some old magazines inside the lid to apply gentle pressure while the glue is drying. Leave to dry for 6–8 hours (or longer, depending on your brand of glue).

7 Insert the glass or Perspex back into the frame, followed by the photograph (face down). Replace the frame back and fasten the clasps.

8 To extend the frame design onto the rest of the box, take a photo of an isolated part of the decorative frame. Scale it down to a size that will fit on the box and print out eight copies on photo paper. Cut out the design and glue it onto the lower corners of each side of the box; if there's room, you could glue detail photos onto the corners of the lid, too.

FURTHER IDEAS

- Instead of paint, cover the box in fabric or decorative paper before fixing on the frame, or use other cut-paper embellishments for decoration.

- Use a plain frame and decorate it with découpage paper or fabric before fixing it in place.

POLAROID HANGING FRAME

Turn a picture frame into a versatile hanging photo display by clipping your favorite Polaroid or Instagram prints onto strung wires. It's simple to swap new favorites in and out when you fancy a change. Use jazzy clips or mini pegs to hold the photos and layer as many as you wish for a totally unique and personalized display.

1 Collect your Polaroids together or print out your Instagram shots. If you have neither, don't panic: there are various apps and online resources that you can use to create Polaroid-style images from your photos (see page 142). Print your photos out on sheets of 6 x 4-in. (15 x 10-cm) glossy photo paper at high print quality (see page 14). Trim the excess paper off up to the edge of the "Polaroid" borders.

2 Remove the back panel of the frame, any paper inside, and the glass or Perspex, leaving you with just the frame. If there are any metal pieces or nails in the frame that are designed to bend and hold the back on, remove those, too.

3 Turn the frame over and lay it on a work surface in the portrait orientation. Down one side, make pencil marks 1¼ in. (3 cm), 8 in. (20 cm), and 14 in. (36 cm) down from the top edge of the aperture. Repeat on the other side of the frame. Line up the staple gun so that the top of the staple is on the first mark, and fire a staple into the frame. Repeat at each marked point. (If your frame is soft wood and the staples go all the way in, screw in small eye hooks instead.)

You will need

- 9 Polaroids (or Instagram prints)
- Photo frame, 16 x 20 in. (40 x 50 cm)
- Craft wire
- 9 decorative paperclips or mini pegs
- Pencil
- Staple gun and staples, or eye hooks
- Wire cutters or pliers with a wire cutter center

Optional (if printing your own photos)

- Printer
- Glossy photo paper, 6 x 4 in. (15 x 10 cm)
- Scissors

Wire tension

Keep equal tension across the three wires; if you're pulling too tight on one, you'll see the other one(s) go loose.

4 Thread the end of your wire through the staple and loop it around, keeping the wire at the top of the staple. Tie it off to secure and trim off the excess with wire cutters.

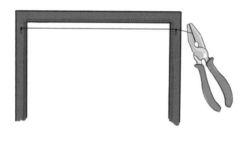

5 Pull the wire gently across the frame and cut, leaving at least 4 in. (10 cm) excess to tie off at the other end. Thread the wire through the corresponding staple. To create tension, grip the end of the wire with the pliers and pull it taut, then lift the pliers to pull the wire back on itself to form a bend in the wire around the staple. Loop the wire around the staple a few times, then tie off and cut off any excess.

6 Repeat steps 4 and 5 on the other two rows of staples.

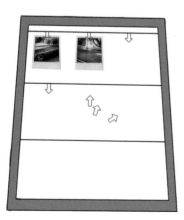

7 Thread three clips onto the top wire. Fix a Polaroid into each clip. Repeat for the remaining rows. Your frame is now ready to hang; alternatively, you can simply prop it up against the wall.

FURTHER IDEAS

- You can use any size frame you like. Just lay the Polaroids over the top first to work out how many rows you need to string.

- Don't stop at just photos—you could add keepsakes to create a memory frame. Tickets and other paper ephemera would work well.

- Super-size it to create a gallery space for your kids' artwork.

- This is a great way to store earrings, too!

- Cover the back panel with decorative paper or collage and insert it into the frame to create a background for your photo display.

Spacing out the Polaroids

If you're working with a different-sized frame, lay out your rows of Polaroids evenly, allowing for the clips, and mark where the wires should go on one side, then transpose those measurements to the other side.

UPCYCLED PHOTO STANDS

It's very simple to create charming photo stands by assembling just a few choice elements. In this case, for my old black-and-white photos, I've selected vintage office rubber stamps with wooden handles as bases and drilled a small hole in the top for the wire, but you could use anything that is stable: small upturned vintage jelly molds, beach pebbles, old-fashioned weights etc. If you can't drill into it, wrap the wire around instead. Use pliers to bend the wire into shapes and simply slot in your prints. As the photos can be changed with ease, you can create temporary displays or even use them as unique place setting card holders for a dinner party.

You will need

- Wire (I used galvanized garden wire approx. ³⁄₆₄ in./1.2mm thick)
- Old office rubber stamps with wooden handle
- All-purpose glue
- Matchbox or similar, to support wire while the glue dries
- Photos
- Wire cutters
- Blunt-nose pliers
- Drill and drill bit at least the diameter of your wire (I used a ³⁄₆₄ in./1.2mm bit)

1 Using wire cutters, cut the wire to about 4 in. (10 cm) in length—longer if you want the stand to be taller. Grip about ½ in. (1 cm) of one end of the wire in the teeth of the pliers and, using your other hand, pull the rest of the wire over the tip of the pliers and down to the left.

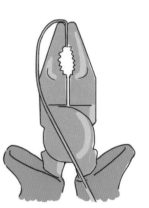

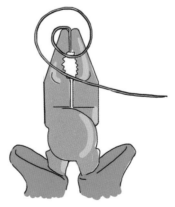

2 Continue pulling the wire round counterclockwise to create a circle and then pull it round an extra quarter circle again. (Imagine the pliers are pointing up to 12 o'clock on a clock face and the wire goes round to 9 o'clock.) Keep it as flat as possible—use the pliers to work the wire if needed.

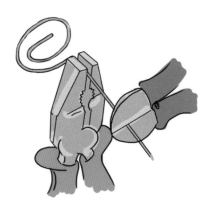

3 Grip the wire at 9 o'clock with the pliers and bend it at a right angle to create the stem. Work the stem straight with the pliers. I cut the wire 1½ in. (4 cm) beyond the right angle, but make it longer if you want a taller stand.

Flattening photographs
Glue aged photographs with curled edges onto card to flatten them down, then trim away any excess card.

4 Select a drill bit the same diameter as (or slightly wider than) your wire and drill into the center of the rubber stamp handle to a depth of about ⅜–⅝ in. (10–15 mm).

5 Apply a small amount of all-purpose glue to the end of the wire and push it into the drilled hole.

6 Lay the stand down flat so that the glue can dry. Keep the wire in a horizontal position by placing a matchbox or something similar underneath it for support until the glue sets.

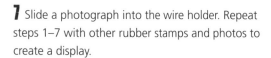

7 Slide a photograph into the wire holder. Repeat steps 1–7 with other rubber stamps and photos to create a display.

FURTHER IDEAS

- Use a vintage salt cellar as a base. They are weighty enough to be stable and the holes in the lid are ready-made. Insert wires of various lengths to create a centerpiece display.

- Experiment with the shapes you bend into the wires: hearts would look lovely for special portrait photo displays, for instance. If you find blunt-nose pliers are too cumbersome, try using long-nose pliers to create more intricate shapes.

- Buy colored craft wires for a different look.

- Let your kids have a go by bending pipe cleaners to hold the photos.

CUT-OUT PHOTO FRAME

Great adventures, vacations, special places—this project shows you how to create a unique piece of art by gathering your best travel photos and cutting a customized mat (mount) for your frame. It's not just for adventurers: you could spell out children's names, feelings, or commemorate special dates (births, weddings, and so on) and show off a collection of treasured images at the same time for a fantastic personalized piece of wall art.

You will need

- Photo frame (mine measured 20 x 9 in./50 x 23 cm)
- Colored card stock (card)
- Plain white office paper
- Photos or copies
- Scissors or craft knife, metal rule, and cutting mat
- Pencil
- Printer
- Eraser
- Repositionable spray adhesive or glue stick

1 Take the frame apart and measure the height and width of the glass. Using a craft knife and metal rule on a cutting mat, cut a piece of colored card stock to the same size. Alternatively, use the glass as a template and draw around it on the colored card stock.

Letter size

For my frame, which was 9 in. (23 cm) tall, three letters approx. 6 in. (15 cm) tall were large enough to reveal enough of the photos but also small enough to leave a border around the edge; you may need to go smaller or use a wider frame for more letters.

2 Use word- or image-processing software to type a letter and/or symbol and scale it up to the required size. Select a font that is thick and/or use a bold font setting (I used Arial Black font in bold at 550 pts size). For shapes, look for "Clip-art" or "Insert Symbol" and adjust the size by increasing the number in the "Font Size" box. Use the rulers at the side of the document to gauge how big you're going. Print the letter/symbol on plain office paper (on a fast, low-quality setting to save ink—see page 14). I needed a heart and the letters N and Y, and used one sheet of paper for each one.

3 Using scissors or a craft knife and metal rule on a cutting mat, carefully cut around the letters.

4 With your colored card stock right side up, lay the letters out, taking care to space them evenly. Starting at one end, hold each letter still as you carefully draw around the outside with a pencil.

5 Using a craft knife on a cutting mat, carefully cut along the pencil marks on the card to create the apertures. Use a metal rule to help you along any straight edges. Remember that you're discarding the letter shapes now and protecting the rest of the card, so place the ruler on the outside of the line so that, if you make an error, it will cut into the letter, which won't matter.

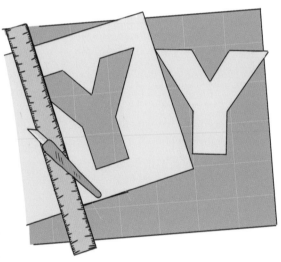

Letter options
If you have a letter such as "A," which has a central section, you can either omit this part of the letter to show more of the photo or cut around that too and set it aside until step 8.

6 Gently rub out any remaining pencil marks with an eraser.

7 Now that your cut-out card is ready, it's time to add your photos. Cut another piece of card (or thick paper) to the size of the glass to use as a base. Place your cut-out card over the base card and lightly draw inside the letters with a pencil, then remove the cut-out card again. Now you can see where to place your images on the base card so that they appear through the cut-out letters. I used one image per letter, but you could create a collage.

8 Once you're happy with the arrangement, mark with pencil around the edges of the photos to create registration marks. Lightly glue the backs of the photos, realign them with the registration marks, and press them firmly into position. Leave to dry. If you have cut-out letter centers set aside, lay the photo card flat, right side up, and align the cut-out card over the top. Lightly glue the backs of the letter centers and press them into position on top of the photos. Leave to dry.

9 Re-assemble the frame, making sure it is clean and dust free first. Replace the glass or Perspex, cut-out card, photo backing card, and then the back of the frame. Clip shut. Now it's ready to hang!

FURTHER IDEAS

- Use colored card and/or colored photos for a striking look. I used yellow because it reminds me of New York taxis, but you can use anything you like.

- The letters can represent anything: places, people, first names, family names, relationships (auntie, grandpa etc.), hobbies, teams, feelings (love), or even a date of birth. Select your photos to complement the theme.

- Forget the frame and laminate your cards together to create personalized name place mats—great for kids!

FOLD-OUT PHOTO ALBUM

This mini album is a great way to group a collection of your favorite images together. Folded up, it's easy to carry around and doesn't need a full battery for you to be able to show it to people. Create an album for an event such as a birthday or holiday, put together a portrait album for the family, or use it as a portfolio for your more arty shots. I've made mine with square-format photos, great for old-fashioned Polaroids or up-to-date Instagram pics, but you can adapt the layout using any shape of photo, as long as they are all the same orientation (i.e. all portrait or all landscape).

You will need

- 12 photos (all same size)
- 4 x 6-in. (10 x 15-cm) photo paper
- Brown paper
- Two coasters from the Card Game (page 63) or two 4-in. (10-cm) square pieces of card stock (card)
- Decorative paper, fabric, or bookbinding fabric
- Sticker or other decorations for cover
- Ribbon
- Printer
- Scissors
- Craft knife, metal rule, and cutting mat
- Repositionable spray adhesive or glue stick
- Old magazines or books to apply pressure
- Pencil

Easy resizing

You don't need to resize your images on the computer. When printing, simply select "4 x 6-in. paper" in the "Page Setup," "Page Layout," or "Media" tab, then select "Scale to Fit Media". Check in the preview window before printing and your photos should have been scaled to the right size for you.

1 Select your images and print them out on 4 x 6-in. (10 x 15-cm) photo paper. Alternatively, order prints from the lab in this size. I used 12 photos in four columns and three rows, but you can use any number as long as the columns are an even number and the rows are an odd number, so that the album will fold correctly.

2 Trim each photo so that it has an even border all around. My borders were approximately ⅛ in. (2 mm) wide and my photos ended up being 3½ in. (9 cm) square, including the borders.

3 Lay out your photos and play around with them to decide on the order. You can group them by color or theme, or randomly. Once you have an order you like, take a quick digital photo of it to keep as reference and help you remember what goes where.

4 Lay your photos out on top of the brown paper. Lay the first photo on the bottom row roughly 2 in. (5 cm) from the left-hand edge of the brown paper, with the factory-cut edge of the paper roll as the bottom edge of your paper. Line up the bottom edges of the bottom row of photos with the bottom edge of the paper, positioning the photos ⅛ in. (2 mm) apart.

5 Cut the brown paper, keeping it larger than your layout. My piece was 20 in. (50 cm) wide by 13¾ in. (35 cm) tall, which allowed roughly 2 in. (5 cm) excess on three sides to trim away later.

6 Take the first photo on the left side of the bottom row, apply glue to the back, and stick it down roughly 2 in. (5 cm) from the left-hand edge of the brown paper, aligning the bottom of the photo with the neat, bottom edge of the paper. Repeat with the other photos in that row, working from left to right and leaving a gap of ⅛ in. (2 mm) between each photo.

7 Repeat for the remaining rows, leaving a gap of 4 mm between each row for folding allowance. Also check that each photo is aligned directly with the photo below it in the column. Cover with a few sheets of clean scrap paper and place heavy magazines or similar on top to apply pressure and keep the paper flat until the glue is dry.

Working with a roll

If you are using brown paper from a roll, use weights to hold down the edges to prevent it from curling up while you work.

8 Using a metal rule and a sharp craft knife on a cutting mat, trim the remaining three edges of the brown paper to the edges of the photos.

9 Fold along the column lines that run top to bottom to create a concertina-style fold.

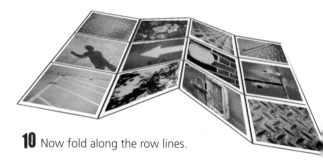

10 Now fold along the row lines.

Neat folds

Place a metal rule in the middle of the gap between the columns and fold the paper over it (or use a bone folder) to get a neat crease.

11 To create the covers, I used two pre-cut card coasters 4 in. (10 cm) square with rounded edges (also used in the Card Game on page 63), but you can cut your own from thick card stock if you prefer. Make sure the cards are ⅜ in. (1 cm) larger all around than your photos.

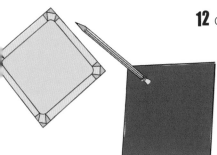

12 Cut a 4¾-in. (12-cm) square of decorative paper, fabric, or book binding material. Apply glue to one side of one card and glue it to the back of the paper in the center, smoothing out any bubbles. Repeat with the other card and let dry. Using a pencil, draw a line at right angles to the edges of the card at the two points on each side where the corner of the card starts to curve. Then at each corner, draw lines coming from the corner at 45 degrees to create a rectangular "tab." Square off the tab.

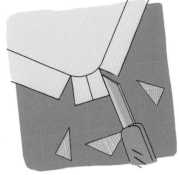

13 Cut away the triangles using the craft knife on a cutting mat. Also cut down the middle of each corner "tab."

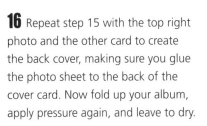

14 Apply glue to the paper around the edge of the card. Pull the paper round over each long straight edge and onto the back of the card. Smooth down. For each corner, pull one half of the tab over at a 45-degree angle (this helps it get round the curved corner), then repeat with the other half of the tab. Press firmly down. Repeat on all corners and on both cards. Leave to dry (apply weight as before).

15 Turn the brown paper sheet over. Using the fold lines as a guide, apply glue to the bottom right square (the back of the bottom left photo if you are looking at it from the front). Lay down the card that you want for the front cover, right side down. Turn the brown paper right side up again and line up the bottom left photo in the center of the card. Press down firmly.

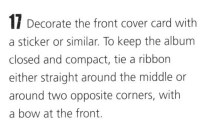

16 Repeat step 15 with the top right photo and the other card to create the back cover, making sure you glue the photo sheet to the back of the cover card. Now fold up your album, apply pressure again, and leave to dry.

17 Decorate the front cover card with a sticker or similar. To keep the album closed and compact, tie a ribbon either straight around the middle or around two opposite corners, with a bow at the front.

FURTHER IDEAS

- Vary the layout: go larger, expand the number of shots, or simply create one long line of images and fold in a concertina style.

- Cut two short lengths of ribbon and fix one end in between the card and the brown paper on each cover when gluing together. Then tie the ribbons together as an alternative way of closing the album.

Chapter 2
Paper Prints

Go beyond the usual and discover how to use your favorite photos to create personalized stationery, hanging decorations, snow globes, and even plant pots! Armed with little more than a pair of scissors and a pot of glue, both kids and grown-ups can enjoy transforming much-treasured paper prints into myriad unusual, inventive, and fun projects.

"EVERYONE'S A STAR" GALLERY

Who doesn't relish seeing the smiling face of a loved one? Celebrate happy times by collecting all of your favorite "Say Cheese!" photos together in one star-filled frame. All you need to create this super-cool artwork are a craft punch, a lick of glue, a frame, and a bunch of good-time photos!

1 Select the photographs you'd like to use, either original prints or copies, and make sure that the images will fit inside the shape and size of the craft punch you're using.

2 Turn the craft punch upside down and insert your photo so that you can see it through the punch hole (you may need to trim the photo for it to fit in the punch). Center the image. Squeeze the punch closed and your cut image will be released. Repeat for each photo.

3 Take the back off the frame. Some frames have a sheet of card or paper already cut to size inside, which can be used for the background; if yours does not, cut some mount board or stiff cardstock to fit inside the frame.

You will need

- Original photos of people or copies (see page 9)
- Mount board or stiff cardstock cut to fit the frame (see step 3)
- Frame
- Craft hole punch (I used a 2-in./5-cm star punch)
- Glue stick
- Paper tissue

Optional

- Ruler

4 Begin to lay out the stars on the mount board or cardstock. I went for a uniform 6 x 6 grid (giving me a total of 36 stars), but go with what works for you and the size of your frame. Keep punching more stars until you have enough. You can arrange them by eye or, if you prefer, measure equal distances between each star with a ruler.

FURTHER IDEAS

- Try different craft-punch shapes (hearts or circles would look good). Alternatively, draw around an object (like a small cookie cutter, for example) to create your shape, then cut out with scissors.

- Experiment with the layout. You don't have to use a grid formation—you could try other arrangements or even spell out words.

5 Once the stars are in position, use a glue stick to apply adhesive to the back of each one in turn, and press firmly into position, using a paper tissue to avoid getting finger marks on the image. As you stick each one down, carefully wipe around the edges with the tissue to remove any excess glue. Repeat until they are all stuck down. Leave to dry.

Removing excess glue
Turn the tissue around in your hand after you've stuck down each image, so that you don't accidentally smear glue onto the next photo, and replace the tissue regularly.

6 Assemble the frame with the sheet of stars and it's ready to hang!

REPURPOSED WATCH KEEPSAKE

In the 16th century, hand-painted miniature portraits were concealed in fine necklaces, rings, and even gentlemen's fob watches worn only by the wealthy. Lockets and keepsakes became hugely popular in the Victorian era, when the advent of photography made them suddenly available to the masses. Soldiers gave them as gifts to faraway sweethearts, babies received them at christenings, and everyone could keep a memento of someone special close to their heart. This project shows you how to repurpose an elegant watch casing into a beautiful, personalized keepsake bracelet for someone special in your life.

You will need

- Wristwatch with clip-on back (see tip)
- Original photos or copies (see page 9)
- Small flat-head screwdriver
- Pencil
- Scissors

1. Measure the face of the watch to work out roughly how big your image needs to be. If you are not using original photos, prepare your digital photograph for printing (see pages 10–12) and scale it to the right size under the "Image Size" tab, or ask your copyshop to reduce or enlarge it for you.

Choosing a watch

Use only broken watches that you no longer want or value. If you are unsure of the value of a watch, get it checked out first. You can also use watches with a "screw-on" type back, but you will need a special tool to open them.

2. Open the watch by inserting the tip of a small flat-head screwdriver into the seam between the watch back and the watch body and gently prising it open. There may be an indent along this seam, which will make this step easier. Remove the back. In most cases, you will simply be able to lift out the watch mechanism. Remove it and set it aside. (See "Choosing a Watch" on page 49 for other types of watch.)

3 Place your photo (or copy) face up on a clean work surface and position the now empty watch over it. You should be able to see through the glass to align your image. Mark around the edge with the pencil. If the glass comes out easily, use that to draw round instead (then replace it). Alternatively, use the watch back as your template.

4 Cut around your pencil line with scissors.

5 Place the photo inside the watch, with the image toward the glass. You may need to keep trimming the edges to get a good fit. Keep turning the watch over to check your results as you work.

6 Once finished, replace the watch back and press closed.

Removing the mechanism
Once the back is removed, you may find that the winding shaft is caught in the hole on the side of the watch. In this case you can either cut the winding shaft off with wire cutters or unscrew the winding cap from the shaft to free and remove the mechanism. Alternatively, leave the mechanism in place but remove the watch hands with long-nose pliers to create a flatter surface for your photo to lie against. Then insert the photo between the face and the glass and press the watch case shut again.

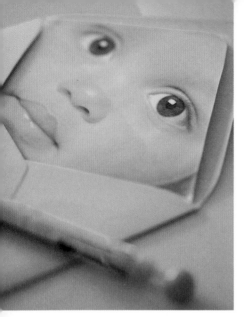

PEEK-A-BOO ENVELOPES

Add a secret surprise to your snail mail by selecting your cutest baby snaps and turning them into envelope inserts—perfect for birth announcements, party invites, or simply just to cheer up someone's day. It would be easy to adapt this project for other occasions, too—for example, use pictures from your wedding day for thank-you notes to guests.

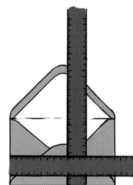

1 Measure your envelope from side to side and take off $\frac{5}{16}$ in. (8 mm) from this measurement to find out how wide your insert needs to be. With the flap of the envelope open, measure from the base of the envelope to near the tip of the flap (just below where the glue line is). Make a note of both measurements.

You will need
- Envelopes
- Digital photos or scans of analog images (or laser copies from a copy shop)
- Plain white office paper
- Ruler
- Printer
- Scissors
- Bone folder
- Scrap paper
- Repositionable spray adhesive, glue stick, or double-sided tape

2 Scale your image to fit this size (see page 12) and print out on plain office paper; alternatively, take your print to a copy shop and have a copy made to the size you need. Try to position the part of the image you want to show near the top of the paper, otherwise it will be hidden inside the envelope. Trim to size.

Which glue?
A glue stick works with thicker paper, but if your paper is thin use spray adhesive to avoid the paper wrinkling—or, if you really don't like glue, use double-sided tape instead.

3 Insert the paper into the envelope, making sure you push it right down to the bottom of the envelope so that it's level on both sides, then fold the flap down. Run the bone folder over the top of the flap to crease the photo. Open the flap and run the bone folder over the crease at the top of the photo to make sure that the crease is nice and sharp.

A rounded tip

If you want to create a rounded tip for your insert, leave a small gap between the folds at the top in step 4 and, when cutting the sections away in step 5, round off the tip with your scissors.

4 Fold the top left-hand corner of the insert back at 45 degrees, until it is just below the glue line, and crease. Repeat with the top right-hand corner. Go over the creases with a bone folder.

5 Cut along the both creases to remove the top left and top right "triangle" sections.

FURTHER IDEAS

- This method works well with other media, such as wrapping paper.

- If you follow steps 1–5, you will have created a template —so why not take that to a copy shop and get a batch of copies printed all at the same time? Then you can just trim and stick them in the envelopes without having to measure and fold each one!

6 Place some scrap paper over the main body of the envelope, then fold the top triangular section of the insert photo down over the scrap paper, separating it from the envelope flap. Apply glue to the back of the insert and then press it back against the envelope flap to secure. Let dry.

CUSTOMIZED NOTEBOOK COVER

Turn a plain notebook into a personalized recipe book by customizing the cover with a shot of your favorite culinary inventions. Get creative and use holiday photos for a travel journal or portraits to make a bespoke diary—the possibilities are endless!

You will need

- Notebook
- Digital photo or scan of analog image
- Photo paper
- Duct tape or bookbinding fabric in a color that complements your image
- Metal rule
- Printer
- Craft knife
- Cutting mat
- Repositionable spray adhesive
- White cotton gloves

1 Measure the front cover of your notebook. Note the measurement from top to bottom, then measure from the right-hand edge of the book up to the point you want your image to end and the spine to start.

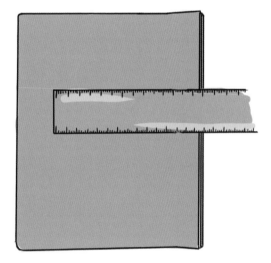

Printing larger

It's ok to print larger than the book if you want to. Just line up the left edge when sticking down and then trim away any excess from the top, right, and bottom edges of your cover. Just bear in mind that you'll trim away some of your image.

2 Make a note of these measurements and resize your image for printing (see page 12). In the printer dialog box, make sure that the "Scale to Fit Media" box is unchecked, so that it prints at the measurements you want. Print out your image on photo paper and let dry.

3 Using a craft knife and metal rule on a cutting mat, trim away the white borders of your print.

4 On a protected surface, apply a light coat of spray adhesive to the back of the print. Wearing white cotton gloves to avoid getting finger marks on the print, align the print with the top, right and bottom edges of the notebook cover and gently smooth down flat.

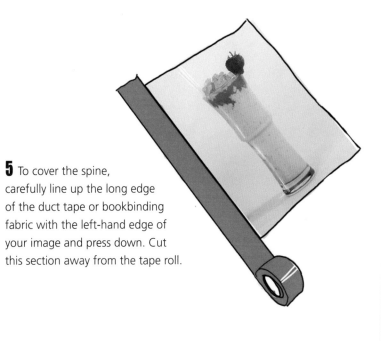

5 To cover the spine, carefully line up the long edge of the duct tape or bookbinding fabric with the left-hand edge of your image and press down. Cut this section away from the tape roll.

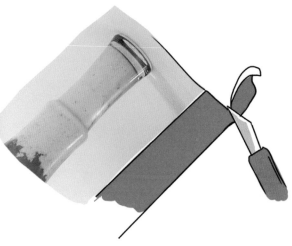

6 Turn the book over, take hold of the other long side of the tape, and gently pull it over the spine and onto the back of the book. Keeping a slight tension here will help the tape wrap around without wrinkling. Press and smooth down. Carefully cut away the excess tape with your craft knife.

FURTHER IDEAS

- To protect your printed cover and to seal in the ink, cover the book with a transparent, self-adhesive plastic film at the end of step 4, before you cover the spine. Lay the book out flat, cut the film larger than the book, cut off each corner at 45 degrees, remove the backing from the film, and smooth the film down over the book, folding the edges over onto the insides of the book cover. Alternatively, spray the image with thin layers of clear varnish and leave to dry before sticking it onto the notebook.

- Skip steps 5 onward and leave the original notebook spine in view. This works really well on notebooks that already have a pretty, patterned cover that complements the colors or theme of your photograph.

Bookbinding fabric
Bookbinding fabric is available in many different colors, comes in self-adhesive rolls or on sheets that you glue in place, and can be cut to whatever dimensions you require. Find it in book-making supply stores (see page 142).

57

PHOTO GIFT TAG

As Mother Teresa said, "It's not how much we give, but how much love we put into giving." Show a loved one your thoughtful side by taking the time to make your own photographic gift tags. This project is quick and very simple, yet really effective. Great for wedding gifts, birthdays, births, and any other memorable occasion—you'll make the recipient feel special before they even open the gift!

You will need

- Photo or print at least 3 in. (7.5 cm) tall by 2 in. (5 cm) wide
- 3-in. (7.5-cm) tag-shaped craft punch (makes 3 x 2-in./7.5 x 5-cm tags)
- Hole punch
- String

Optional

- Spray varnish (if you are using inkjet prints)
- Card stock (card)
- Repositionable spray adhesive or glue stick

1 Select your photos or print out copies that are at least 3 in. (7.5 cm) tall by 2 in. (5 cm) wide. If you are using inkjet prints, spray them with three light coats of varnish, letting each coat dry before you apply the next one.

Making tags stronger
If you want to make your tag more robust, punch out a tag shape from plain card stock and glue it to the back of the photo tag with spray adhesive or a glue stick. Leave to dry.

2 Turn the tag-shaped craft punch upside down and insert your photo so that you can see it through the punch hole (you may need to trim the photo for it to fit in the punch). Center the image. Squeeze the punch closed and your cut image will be released.

3 Take the hole punch and line it up near the top of the tag, centered on the width. Punch a hole for the string.

4 Cut a 10-in. (25-cm) length of string and tie ends together to form a loop. Hold the knot in one hand and find the centerpoint of the loop. Push this point halfway through the punched hole from front to back, then feed the knot through the loop and gently pull tight.

FURTHER IDEAS

- Fix hole strengtheners (available from stationery stores) around the punched hole for robustness.

- Thread the tags with pretty ribbon instead of string. Add beads for decoration.

- Punch out plain colored card or acetate tags for writing on and layer them up over or on the back of the photo tag.

COOKIE CUTTER PHOTO DECORATIONS

Cookie cutters come in many shapes and sizes. By adding a photograph and some pretty ribbon, it's easy to turn them into sweet and sentimental hanging decorations. Pick festive photos for the holidays and embellish with glitter, or use family snaps for a year-round display.

1 Select the cookie cutters you want to use and measure them from top to bottom and from side to side. Make a note of these measurements.

2 Decide which photograph to use in each cutter (a photo of somebody standing would suit a tall, slim-shaped cutter, for example). Refer to your measurements from step 1, resize your photos or copies, if you need to (see page 12), and print out on photo paper. Check that the photos are the correct size by laying the cutters in position over the top before proceeding.

3 Use spray adhesive or a glue stick to coat the backs of the photos with glue, then stick them down on card stock for extra strength. Leave to dry.

4 Cut about 16 in. (40 cm) of ribbon for each cutter frame. Thread the ribbon through the cookie cutter, bring the ends back together, and lift up. The cutter should naturally fall to hang from the center of your ribbon "loop." At this point, tie a double knot in the ribbon so that it sits at the top of the cookie cutter, pulling it tight against the metal as you do so. Now bring the two loose ends of ribbon together again and tie a double knot at that end, too. Tidy up any uneven ribbon ends by trimming across both ends at a 45-degree angle.

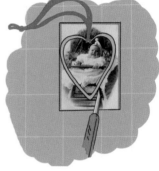

5 Apply clear all-purpose glue very carefully to the edge of your cookie cutter and gently place it down over the photo, keeping the part of the photo you want to display inside the cookie cutter. Press firmly and leave to dry. You may want to place a heavy book over the cutter to apply pressure while the glue dries.

6 Using a craft knife on a cutting mat, carefully cut around the outside edge of the cookie cutter to remove the excess photo and card. Take care not to apply too much pressure to the cutter as you work to avoid breaking the glue seal.

Alternative method

If you're not confident about using a craft knife (as is used in step 6), after step 4 align your cutter over your photograph and draw around the outside of the cutter with a sharp pencil. Cut carefully along this line with scissors, then follow step 5 to complete your decoration.

FURTHER IDEAS

- Instead of aluminum cutters, use brightly colored plastic cookie cutters, or paint your own with enamel paint.

- Before you tie the loose ends of the ribbon together, thread on some decorative beads.

- Embellish both the photo and the cutter with glitter for some festive sparkle.

CARD GAME

A fun way to show off your favorite vacation snaps is to turn them into a "find the pair" memory card game. Cover the backs in a pretty paper with a small repeating pattern so that they all look the same—then no-one can cheat! You could adapt the project by laminating the images first and sticking them to pre-cut cork coaster bases to create a personalized set of drinks mats for your home.

You will need

- At least 12 card drinks mats, 4 in. (10 cm) square
- Gift wrap or decorative paper, preferably with a small, repeating pattern
- Digital photos or scans of analog images
- Scrap paper
- Repositionable spray adhesive
- Craft knife, metal rule, and cutting mat
- Scissors

1 Protect your work surface with scrap paper, then spray one side of the drinks mat with spray adhesive. Stick it down on the back of the decorative paper, aligning one edge with the factory-cut edge of the paper. Repeat all along the edge of the paper. The aim is to have all the backs looking the same when the cards are all face down, so align the pattern as uniformly as possible.

2 Using a craft knife and metal rule on a cutting mat, carefully cut around the edge of each card.

Consistent card backs

Cut across the decorative paper in a straight line at the same point in the pattern repeat as on the factory-cut edge and use this to align and glue the next row of cards. Then all the backs will look the same.

3 Select your photographs and print them out at 4¼ in. (10.5 cm) square on photo paper (see page 12). Print each one on a sheet of 4 x 7-in. (13 x 18-cm) photo paper—or print several at a time on US letter size (A4) paper. Print two copies of each image. Trim away any excess with scissors.

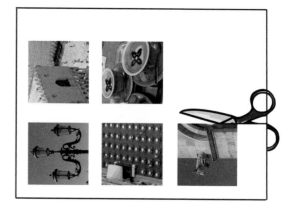

4 On a protected surface, lightly spray the back of the photo with spray adhesive. On a clean surface, place the photo face down, then put the card on top, uncovered side down and centering it on the back of the photo. Make sure that both the photo and the decorative paper pattern are the right way up. Press firmly and leave to dry.

5 Using a craft knife and metal rule on a cutting mat, carefully trim away the excess paper from the edge of the card.

FURTHER IDEAS

- Make or decorate a box to keep the cards in or to give as a gift. Alternatively, you could tie the cards together with a decorative ribbon.

- Cover the cards with self-adhesive clear plastic for durability.

CRAZY HAIR PLANT POTS

As a child, did you ever paint a face on an eggshell and grow cress for hair? This grown-up twist on a classic kids' craft takes some basic plant pots, gives them a shot of color, and personalizes them with faces from your photo collection. Add herbs or plants for instant "hair." It's a fun project to make for, or with, your children: give them a pot each to show them how to nurture their own plant (or "hairstyle"). Alternatively, gift wrap each with a handy packet of seeds tucked inside for a really thoughtful present for budding gardeners of all ages.

You will need

- Ceramic plant pots—I used 2½ in. (6 cm) tall pots for seedlings, but any size will work
- Digital photos, or scans of analog images, of children's faces
- Photo paper
- Decorator's clear varnish
- Compost
- Small plant or seeds
- Ruler
- Printer
- Scissors
- White cotton glove
- Clear all-purpose glue
- Brush

Optional

- Spray enamel paint (to paint pots)

1 Measure the height of the pots from top to bottom. If the pot has a rim, measure from just below the rim to the base. Note this measurement.

2 If you wish, spray the pots with enamel spray paint. Several thin, light coats are better than one heavy coat, which might run. Leave to dry. If the pot has a drainage plate, paint that, too.

3 Resize your photo so that the measurement from the chin to halfway up the forehead of the subject is just smaller than the height of the pot (measured in step 1).

4 To adjust the color, play with the "Hue," "Variations," or "Tint" options in your editing software (see pages 11–12). I changed the photos to match the color of the pots, but you could try complementary colors or leave them a natural skin tone, if you prefer.

5 Print out on photo paper at high quality (see page 14) and leave to dry for half an hour.

6 Using scissors, carefully cut around the outline of the face, then cut across the forehead in a straight line.

7 Wearing a white cotton glove to protect the print, apply glue to the back of the face and stick it onto the pot, lining up the top of the image with the top of the pot (or just below the rim if the pot has one).

8 Brush on a layer of clear decorator's varnish and leave to dry. Repeat for increased water resistance. Fill with compost and plant a cutting or seeds to create the "hair."

FURTHER IDEAS

- For patient kids, plant seeds in soil and watch them grow.

- Make some for the grown-ups, too, to make a plant-pot family. Just use bigger pots and scale up the faces to fit.

"UNDER THE SEA" PHOTO GLOBE

Snow globes don't have to only make an appearance during the festive season. Using a glass jar, a photo, and an ornament for an aquarium, make an "Under the Sea" scene instead. Shake it to see blue and green glitter fall gently down, and get a glimpse into your own underwater world.

You will need

- Glass jar with lid (select one that looks nice upside down—honey jars are good)
- Small ornament for an aquarium
- Print or digital photo
- Small self-adhesive laminating card for making ID badges (available from stationers)
- Distilled water (enough to overfill the jar)
- Glycerin (available from craft and baking stores)
- Extra-fine blue, light green, and green glitter
- Clear silicon sealant
- Ruler or tape measure
- Scissors
- Bone folder
- Glue gun
- Teaspoon
- Plastic container or sink

Optional (if printing your photos)
- Photo paper
- Printer

1 Empty and clean the glass jar and lid. With the jar upside down, measure the height of the jar.

2 Select an ornament and check that it will fit inside the jar and within the lid. I chose a plastic seaweed ornament from an aquatic pet shop (as it is already waterproof and complements my "under the sea" design) and trimmed it to fit, but you could use anything that will not deteriorate in liquid, such as plastic flowers and figurines.

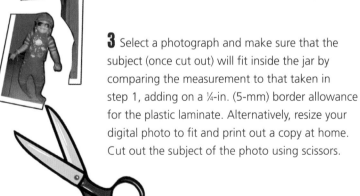

3 Select a photograph and make sure that the subject (once cut out) will fit inside the jar by comparing the measurement to that taken in step 1, adding on a ¼-in. (5-mm) border allowance for the plastic laminate. Alternatively, resize your digital photo to fit and print out a copy at home. Cut out the subject of the photo using scissors.

4 Place the cut-out photo in the center of a self-adhesive laminating card, remove the protective cover, and smooth the laminating card closed to seal the image. Alternatively, take your cut-out photo to a copy shop and ask them to laminate it for you.

5 Get rid of any air bubbles by pressing on the plastic around the edges of your photo with a bone folder.

6 Leave the base of the laminated photo intact until just below the bottom of your photograph. From that point upward, cut around the photo, leaving a border of at least ¼ in. (5 mm) of clear plastic.

7 Place the cut-out photo face down on your work surface. Place a ruler across the base, just below the photo, and run the pointed end of a bone folder or an old credit card along the edge of the ruler to score a fold line. With the photo facing forward, fold the base of the photo back at a right angle. Place the base inside the jar lid and trim off any excess laminate until it fits inside the lid.

8 Place the jar lid upside down (if it has a bar code or similar on its side edge, turn this to the back, out of sight). Using the glue gun, apply glue to the base of the laminated photo and stick it inside the lid, with the photo facing forward and the base positioned in the front half of the lid.

Glitter and glycerin

Add more glycerin or glitter if required, depending on the size of your jar and the effect you want. Go easy on the glitter, though, as too much may obscure the photograph once shaken.

9 Now apply more glue to the base of the ornament and fix it down in the middle of the lid, behind the photo. Check to make sure the glass jar can still screw into the lid. Set the lid aside to dry completely overnight.

10 Fill the jar roughly three-quarters full with distilled water (normal tap water is less pure and will go cloudy over time). Add one teaspoon of glycerin, which makes the glitter stay suspended in the liquid for longer once the globe is shaken, and stir it into the water. Add a small shake each of extra-fine blue, light green, and emerald green glitter. Stir it all up with the teaspoon.

11 Now place the jar in a plastic container or over the sink and top it up with more distilled water until the jar is completely full.

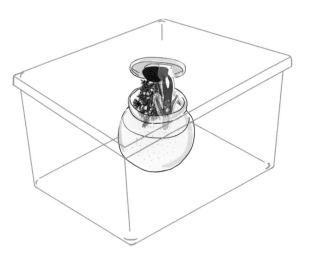

12 As some jars have visible seams in the glass, turn the jar so that the seams are at the sides and the front of the glass is clear. Hold the lid so that the photo is facing you, so that it will align with the clear glass. Now place the lid back onto the jar—some water will be displaced and will spill over the edge into the plastic container or sink. Screw the lid on tight and leave to dry.

FURTHER IDEAS

- You don't have to use an ornament: try laminating two photos together or gluing in a few different ones to create a double-sided photo globe.

- Decorate around the lid with a ribbon or a gift tag, or spray the lid with colored enamel paint.

- Use snow for festive versions, or try plastic figurines or decorations to create other themes.

- Add a drop of blue food coloring for bluer water.

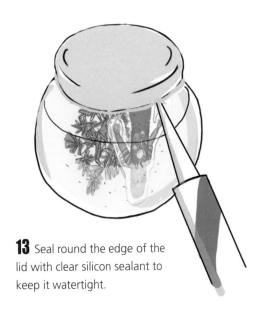

13 Seal round the edge of the lid with clear silicon sealant to keep it watertight.

"WATCH THE BIRDIE" MOBILE

This papercraft project is very versatile, because you can use any kind of photograph you like. I used abstract, night-time shots from a road trip backed with silver card, so the birds remind me of the freedom of travel, but you could use family portraits with bright colored card for a nursery mobile or black-and-white images with neon decorative card for a mobile with maximum impact. Select your photos and card to suit your own home style and watch your photos take flight!

1 Trace the bird body and the wing templates onto the card stock and cut around them with scissors. Using a metal rule and craft knife on a cutting mat, cut the lines in the tail and wings and the slit across the body. Use the safety pin and a bradawl or knitting needle to make the eye hole in the template.

2 Place the bird body card template on the back of the the silver card and draw around it six times to create six bird outlines. Repeat with the wing template to create six wing shapes. Cut these shapes out with scissors.

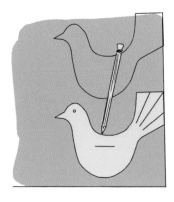

You will need

- US letter size (A4) card stock (card) for the template
- Stiff silver card stock (card)
- 9 photos measuring at least 5 x 7 in. (13 x 18 cm) or copies (see page 9)
- Gray cotton thread or string
- Silver embroidery floss (thread) or decorative ribbon for hanging branch
- Branch roughly 30 in. (80 cm) long
- Templates on pages 140–1
- Tracing paper
- Pencil
- Scissors
- Metal rule, craft knife, and cutting mat
- Safety pin
- Bradawl or knitting needle
- Repositionable spray adhesive

3 Turn one photo image side down. Spray the back of the bird body card shape with spray adhesive and press it down onto the back of the photo, lining up the right-angled shape of the bird tail with the top right corner of the photo print. Using a craft knife on a cutting mat, carefully cut away the excess photo.

4 Place the template over the silver side of the bird again. With the pencil, mark the eye hole and the slit in the body on the silver card below. For the tail, holding the template in place, gently lift the tail flaps and draw the cut lines on the silver card below. Using the craft knife and ruler, cut along the new belly and tail lines on the bird body.

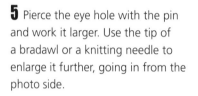

Cutting out the birds

If you are using card with a design or color on one side only, draw around three bodies and wings one way round, then flip the template over and draw the other three bodies and wings. Stick your photos to the non-decorated side of the card.

5 Pierce the eye hole with the pin and work it larger. Use the tip of a bradawl or a knitting needle to enlarge it further, going in from the photo side.

6 Turn the photo over so that the bird is silver side up. Holding the craft knife flat, carefully saw away the rough card from around the eye hole.

7 You can fit two wings on one 5 x 7-in. (13 x 18-cm) photo. Glue the silver card wing to the back of the photo and cut out the wing shape. Reposition the template on the silver side of the wing. Gently lift the flaps and draw the cut lines on the silver card below. Then cut along them, using the craft knife and ruler.

8 With the wing silver side up and the cut in the center facing the head of the bird, gently feed the wing through the slit in the bird's body. When it's halfway through, slide the wing forward so that the body slots into the central slit to hold the wing in place.

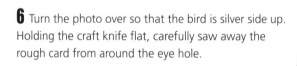

9 Pierce a hole in the tail with the pin, then thread cotton through the bird's eye and the hole in the tail. Tie at the top to form a triangle (this ensures that the bird will hang in a balanced position and not tilt) and leave about 3 ft (90 cm) excess cotton for hanging.

10 Repeat steps 3–9 to make five more birds. When spraying the silver bird bodies with spray adhesive in step 3, spray three one way and three the other to create birds flying in different directions.

11 Wrap the silver embroidery floss (thread) around one end of the clean branch and tie off. Leave as much excess as you need for hanging, then tie off the other end of the thread at the other end of the branch.

12 Hang the branch up where you can reach it and begin to attach the birds. Starting on the left, hold the first bird 12 in. (30 cm) down from the branch. Wrap the excess cotton around the branch a short way in from the end just a few times for now, so that the bird stays in position. Repeat with the remaining birds, spacing them evenly along the branch and hanging them at distances of 24 in. (60 cm), 16 in. (40 cm), 32 in. (80 cm), 20 in. (50 cm), and 12 in. (30 cm) below the branch.

13 Once you're happy with the layout, tie off each thread in a double knot and trim off the excess.

Vary the birds
The birds are designed so that, if the bird rotates when hung, a photo is always visible on either the body or the wings. Add variety by folding some wings upward or splaying some of the "feathers" in the wings and tail.

FURTHER IDEAS

- Spray paint the branch first, or wrap it entirely in a colorful yarn for a less rustic look.

- Add in other elements (such as feathers) by tying them onto cotton and tying the other end of the cotton onto the branch.

- Instead of using silver card, glue two photos back to back for a double-sided photo feast.

GLASS TABLE-TOP DISPLAY

Perfect for those who live in small spaces, have run out of walls to hang art on, or just like their furniture to be that bit more interesting, this project converts a basic glass-topped table into a custom photo-gallery-come-picture-frame. Celebrate your family history by dusting off those old snapshots languishing in a shoebox somewhere and displaying them for all to see. The contents of the display can be easily changed and the photos remain protected from dust and scratches. Give the rest of the table a lick of paint to complete the look.

You will need

- Self-assembly glass-topped table
- Paint for wood
- Clear acrylic sheet 1/16 in. (1 mm) thick
- Selection of photographs or copies (see page 8)
- Photo mounts or low-tack double-sided tape
- Paintbrush
- Sandpaper
- Marker pen
- Metal rule, craft knife, and cutting mat

1 Assemble the table (without the glass) and give it a coat of paint all over, except for the grooves where the glass slides in. Leave to dry. Apply a second coat of paint if required and leave to dry.

2 Now remove one side of the table. Sand the grooves for the glass with sandpaper to remove any errant paint and to make them slightly larger.

3 Lay the acrylic sheet out flat. Place the glass from the table on top of the acrylic, lining up two edges. Using a marker pen, draw around the remaining edges to copy the shape of the glass onto the acrylic.

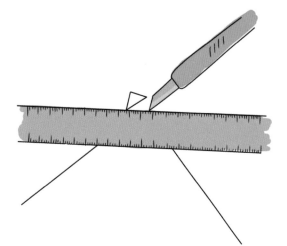

4 Set the glass to one side. Using a metal rule and craft knife on a cutting mat, cut along your marks to cut out the acrylic. Lay the acrylic over the glass to check that they are exactly the same size. If they are not, re-mark and re-cut. Set the acrylic aside.

5 Start to arrange the photos around the edge of the glass, lining the straight edges up with the straight edges of the glass, but leaving a border of roughly ⅛ in. (3 mm) all the way around (which will help the glass fit in later). Leave a larger border if you want a frame of clear glass to be visible around your photo collection. Then fill in the center with photos until the whole area is covered. Take a digital photo for reference, if required.

Tabletops

I used an inexpensive self-assembly glass-topped table, which comes with glass and fixings included. For the acrylic sheet that covers the photos, I dismantled a cheap picture frame and used the acrylic "glass." Alternatively, you can buy acrylic sheets from craft stores and online.

6 Working from one corner to another, lift off one photo, apply photo mounts or low-tack double-sided tape to the back, and stick the photograph back down on the glass. Use extra mounts for old photos that have curled edges.

7 Remove the protective film from one side of the acrylic sheet (if present) and place that side down over the photographs, keeping the area free from dust. Peel back the protective film from the other side by about ¾ in. (2 cm) all the way around.

8 Holding the acrylic and the glass together in your hands, begin to feed it into the grooves of the table, photo side up. Slide it in all the way. (If there's resistance, slide the acrylic in first and then the glass. If it still resists, sand the grooves a bit more.)

9 Replace the last side of the table, making sure that the acrylic and glass fit inside the groove. Gently screw the section in place. Once the table is assembled, you can remove the remaining protective film from the acrylic to reveal your completed project.

FURTHER IDEAS

- Replace the photographs with slides or other transparency-based prints and place a light source on the table shelf below for an impromptu lightbox display.

- Select one favorite photograph for the center and use a decorative paper or film for a border.

- Enlarge a single photograph to fill the entire top.

REPURPOSED VINTAGE PAPER PRINT

A simple way to give a photograph some depth and context and turn it into a personalized artwork is to use vintage paper, in this case a musical score, as a background and then print your image over the top using a home printer. Print black-and-white or color photos directly onto the paper; alternatively print onto inkjet acetate sheets that can then be layered over collages or larger backgrounds. Any decorative paper can be used as a background—musical scores, maps, pages from broken large books, such as encyclopedias or dictionaries. Even thin papers such as newspaper print can work—just back them with a sheet of ordinary office paper for strength first.

Converting a photo to black and white

You can use software (Image > Adjust > Desaturate) before printing. Alternatively, you can send to print in color and tick the "Grayscale Printing" box (or similar) in the printer dialog box—the printer will then print in black and white only.

You will need

- Digital photo or scan of analog image
- Vintage paper
- US letter size (A4) office paper
- Frame
- Pencil
- Craft knife, metal rule, and cutting mat
- Printer

Optional

- Sheet of clear acetate for inkjet printers

1 Prepare your photograph by sizing it to your requirements—up to a maximum of US letter size (A4) (see page 12). If you want more of the vintage paper to be visible, select an image with a pale or white background (because less ink will be deposited, allowing the vintage paper to show through), use the "Dodge" tool in photo software to lighten certain areas (see page 12), or "cut out" your subject (page 10). To leave borders/space around your printed image, make the image smaller and make sure that the "Scale to Fit Media" box is not checked and the scale is showing as 100% before sending to print.

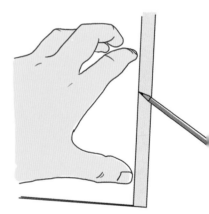

2 To fit the vintage paper through your printer you may need to trim it. Lay a piece of US letter size (A4) paper over your vintage paper and center it. Holding the paper flat, draw around it with a pencil.

3 Using a craft knife and metal rule on a cutting mat, trim along your pencil lines to remove the excess.

4 Feed the vintage paper into your printer and print your image directly onto it. Alternatively, if you prefer to only use products recommended by your printer manufacturer, print your image onto a clear sheet of inkjet acetate instead and lay this over your vintage paper. Now frame and enjoy!

Attaching acetate

Use glue dots or photo mounts in the corners to stick the acetate sheet onto a larger piece of vintage paper.

FURTHER IDEAS

- Print your photos onto acetate sheets for inkjets to build up layers and create a composite design. With this method, you are no longer limited to paper that can absorb ink, so shiny gift wrap and other plastic-based patterned paper can be used, too (or even a collage of tickets or other paper ephemera).

- For colored paper backgrounds (such as maps), a black-and-white photograph works best—but experiment and see what works for you.

Chapter 3
Image Transfer

No longer do you have to restrict yourself to printing your favorite photos on paper! This chapter sets out simple techniques for transferring your images onto a multitude of different surfaces, including leather, wood, ceramic, and fabric, allowing you to create unique, personalized gifts and items for your home.

TRANSFER TOTE BAG

Tote bags are practical, but they don't have to be boring! Use iron-on transfer paper to create a personalized letter design from your photos. Any white on the photo becomes transparent when transferred in this manner, so it is best to use a white tote. I've used a shot of a bunch of roses, but it could be sunsets, people, pets—anything you like!

You will need

- Digital photo or scan of analog image
- Lesley Riley's Transfer Artist Paper (TAP) (see page 142)
- US letter size (A4) plain office paper
- Plain white tote bag
- Inkjet printer
- Scissors
- Pencil
- Iron and ironing board
- Soft cloth for ironing

Optional

- Tweezers

1 Using photo-editing software, scale your image to the desired size (see page 12). Using one sheet of TAP paper, white side up, and following the manufacturer's instructions (the printer settings required are usually "plain paper" and "mid-range quality"), print out your image.

Paper sizes

TAP paper comes in US letter format, which is very similar in size to the A4 paper commonly used in the UK and Europe. (US letter size is 8½ x 11 in./216 x 279.4 mm; A4 is approx. 8¼ x 11¾ in./210 x 297 mm.) Most printers in the UK and Europe have a US letter setting as well as A4.

2 Using photo-editing software, type the letter you wish to use—this will be your template. I made mine US letter (A4) size, so that it would reveal more of the photo. Print the letter out on plain paper, then cut it out. (You could also cut away the letter and use the remaining border as your template. In step 3, this allows you to place the "letter" over your TAP photo print and move it around to select the section of the photo that you want to see through the "window.")

Using layers

If you are familiar with using layers in photo-editing software, skip steps 2–3 and layer your transparent letter over your image, then print. This will save your ink.

3 Place the letter template flat over the TAP photo print you printed in step 1. (If the letter is asymmetrical, turn your template over so that, once transferred to the bag, the letter comes out the right way round.) Carefully draw around the edge of the letter to transfer the shape to the photo. Then carefully cut along this line to create your photo letter on the TAP photo print.

4 Lay the tote bag out flat on an ironing board. Place the photo letter in the center of the bag, printed side down. (If your letter is asymmetrical, then the letter shape should look the right way round again when you look at the back of the TAP photo print.)

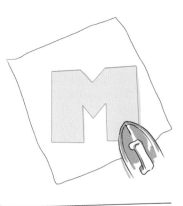

5 Place a thin cloth on top of the paper to protect both your iron plate and the bag. With a pre-heated dry iron (no steam) on a very hot setting, hold the letter down in one corner and press the iron down over the opposite corner. Gently move the iron around, pressing firmly. Once the transfer has taken place, the backing paper will lift away. You cannot "over-iron" the paper, but take care not to scorch the fabric.

6 Peel the transfer paper away while it is still hot; you may wish to use tweezers to do this. Test one corner first: if the white side of the TAP is smooth, the transfer is complete; if it is not smooth, carefully replace and apply more heat, pressing firmly. Once the transfer paper is removed, let the fabric cool.

FURTHER IDEAS

- Not only can you apply this method to T-shirts, baby grows, bibs, aprons and tea towels, but these transfer sheets also work on wood, glass, canvas, metal and polymer clay!

- Skip the letter part and print a whole photo onto your bag! (Print the TAP in mirror image.) You can even draw on the TAP paper, too.

- Experiment with using different-colored fabric underneath your transfer for interesting effects.

EMBROIDERY HOOP FRAMES

Embroidery hoops are traditionally used to hold fabric taut for fine needlework, and come in a wide range of sizes and colors. Using cotton canvas and an inkjet printer, you can create personalized wall art by repurposing these hoops into eye-catching frames to create a talking point on your wall.

You will need

- Embroidery hoops in various sizes and colors
- Digital photos or scans of analog images
- Cotton canvas sheets for inkjet printers (not canvas paper)
- Tape measure or ruler
- Inkjet printer
- Small scissors

Optional

- Paint and paintbrush
- Varnish

1 Measure your embroidery hoops and make a note of the diameters. If you are using a US letter-size (A4) printer, use hoops with a diameter of 6¾ in. (17 cm) or less, so that there will be enough canvas around the edges of the images to be trapped between the hoops and hold everything in place. If you wish, paint wooden hoops in bright colors, using acrylic paint or matchpot paint samples, and seal with varnish once dry.

Saving space
Print large and small images side by side on the same page to make your canvas go further.

2 Prepare your digital photograph for printing (see page 12). Make sure that the shortest side is at least ¾ in. (2 cm) larger than the diameter of your hoop. If it is not, scale it up to the required size.

3 In your printer dialog box, select "Borderless Printing" if the image is large and may be cropped by the printer. Print the image out on a sheet of cotton canvas for inkjet printers (make sure you use canvas and not canvas-effect paper, which would crease). Leave to dry for two hours before handling.

4 Loosen the hoop fastening (you can take if off completely if you wish) and separate the adjustable outer hoop from the inner hoop. Set aside.

5 Remove the backing from your canvas (if it has one).

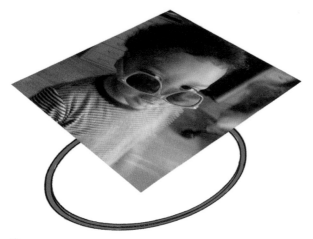

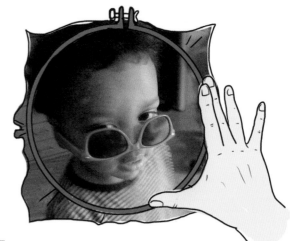

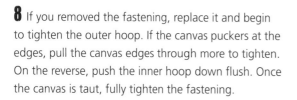

6 Lay the inner hoop flat on your work surface, then lay the canvas on top, print side up, with the image centered over the hoop. Adjust if necessary, but remember to leave a border of at least ¾ in. (2 cm) all around.

7 Keeping the canvas stretched across the inner hoop, open out the outer hoop and bring it down over the canvas and inner hoop (rather like putting an elastic band over fabric at the top of a jam jar).

8 If you removed the fastening, replace it and begin to tighten the outer hoop. If the canvas puckers at the edges, pull the canvas edges through more to tighten. On the reverse, push the inner hoop down flush. Once the canvas is taut, fully tighten the fastening.

FURTHER IDEAS

- Cross-stitch through the canvas and create custom embellishments on top of your images with brightly colored embroidery floss (thread).

- Group lots of different sizes and colors together on the wall for maximum impact.

- Use any subject matter you like—get creative!

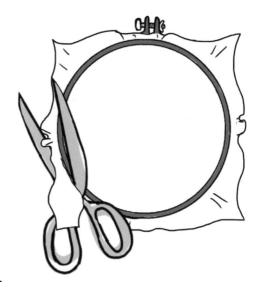

9 Using small scissors, trim away any excess canvas from the back of the hoop.

WATER SLIDE DECAL TEA CUP

Transform plain vases, old china, even ceramic tiles, and add your own embellishments to vintage plates for a spot of upcycling. This simple project shows you how to use your favorite images to decorate the outside of ceramic cups and saucers with a little more finesse. You can use full-color images or black-and-white, and include text or even bands of pattern that wrap around the cup. The technique also works on candles and soap—but don't put those in the oven!

You will need

- White cup and saucer
- Digital photo or scan of analog image
- Clear water slide decal paper for inkjet printers (see page 142)
- Clear spray varnish
- Tape measure or ruler
- Inkjet printer
- Scissors
- Bowl of warm water
- Sponge
- Oven

1 Measure the area on the cup and saucer that you want to decorate. Resize your images to these dimensions (see page 12). I made my image for the cup larger than the one for the saucer.

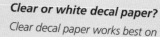

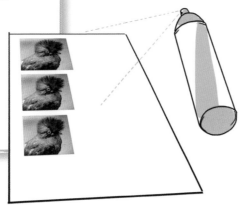

Clear or white decal paper?

Clear decal paper works best on white ceramics; if your ceramic surface is a darker color, opt for white decal paper. Decal paper is also available for laser printing.

2 Use your inkjet printer to print out your image on the decal paper, following the paper manufacturer's instructions. Allow to dry for at least 30 minutes.

3 Spray the decal paper with clear varnish to seal in the ink. Give it three quick coats separated by 10–15-minute intervals. Avoid using too much varnish, as it will stiffen the decal. Leave to dry.

4 Cut around the edge of the design for the tea cup with the scissors. Make sure you cut right to the edge of your image to avoid white borders showing.

Treat with care!
Handwash instead of using a dishwasher to extend the life of your decals.

5 Submerge the decal in a bowl of warm water for 15–30 seconds until the decal slides off the paper. Do not try to force the decal off the paper prematurely, as it may rip.

FURTHER IDEAS

- Create custom coasters by applying your decals to plain white tiles and sticking felt to the back to protect your table from scratches.

- Apply to glassware rather than ceramics, which would have a result similar to the Vellum Tealights on page 118, although the decals are not translucent.

6 Slide the decal off the backing paper and onto your cup. For larger decals, start at one edge and slowly peel away the backing paper as you go. It won't stick immediately, so you can gently move it around if needs be. Use the sponge to smooth away any bubbles and squeeze the water out from under the decal so it sticks well.

7 Repeat steps 4–6 with the saucer. Preheat the oven to 230–266°F (110–130°C/Gas ¼–½).

8 Once you have applied your decals, place the ceramics into the oven for 10–15 minutes to harden. Alternatively, leave the ceramics overnight and then coat with clear varnish to seal, covering the decal and going slightly over the edges onto the surrounding ceramic.

LEATHER GADGET CASE

This project shows you how to correctly size and sew a simple yet sturdy case for your phone (or other gadgets) using leather off-cuts. You can then use a straightforward image-transfer technique to personalize the case with your own photograph. It's a fantastic antidote to homogeneous, mass-produced cases and should bring a smile every time it's handled (which, for phones, is pretty often). Once you get going, you may find yourself making more for friends and family, each one unique and special. Scale up for larger gadgets, such as tablets, or lengthen the case to house eyeglasses (spectacles) or sunglasses.

You will need

- Card stock (card)
- White leather off-cuts
- Digital photo or scan of analog image
- Dark T-shirt image transfer sheets for inkjet printer
- Strong thread
- Pencil and ruler
- Sharp scissors
- Inkjet printer
- Iron
- Small bulldog clips
- Sharp needle for leather
- Thimble

1 Place your gadget on the card stock and draw around it. Now extend the bottom and sides by ⅜ in. (1 cm) to allow for the thickness of the gadget and stitching. In the bottom two corners, draw a curved line ⅜ in. (1 cm) out that follows the corners of your gadget. Cut out your template with scissors.

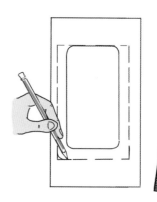

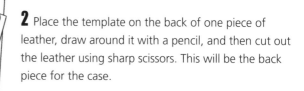

2 Place the template on the back of one piece of leather, draw around it with a pencil, and then cut out the leather using sharp scissors. This will be the back piece for the case.

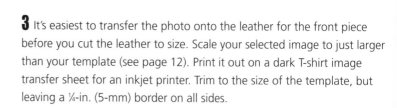

3 It's easiest to transfer the photo onto the leather for the front piece before you cut the leather to size. Scale your selected image to just larger than your template (see page 12). Print it out on a dark T-shirt image transfer sheet for an inkjet printer. Trim to the size of the template, but leaving a ¼-in. (5-mm) border on all sides.

4 Turn your iron to its hottest setting, with no steam. Let it warm up for 5–8 minutes. Place a piece of card stock flat on a solid surface with the leather on top, right side up. Peel the backing paper away from your transfer and lay it flat on the leather, image side up.

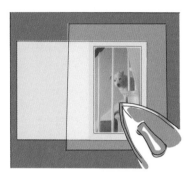

5 Place the sheet of protective paper that comes inside packs of dark T-shirt transfer paper over the image and iron up and down and from side to side, applying pressure and keeping the iron moving, for approx. 30 seconds (refer to your paper manufacturer's instructions), taking care not to scorch the leather. Let cool. Remove the protective paper.

Preventing mirror images
When printing, if you select the media/paper type as "T-Shirt Transfers" (or similar), your printer may automatically flip your photo over into mirror image (which is required when using LIGHT T-shirt image transfer sheets). However, we're using DARK T-shirt image transfer sheets, which do not need to be mirror image.
If this happens and you don't want it to, flip the image yourself before sending to print, then the printer will flip it back the right way again.

6 Center the card template on the photo-transferred leather and draw around it with a pencil. Use sharp scissors to cut it out. This is the front piece of the case.

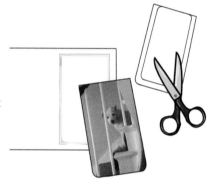

7 Place the back leather piece right side down with the front leather piece right side up on top, aligning the edges carefully. Clip the two pieces together, using the small bulldog clips to keep them in position while you sew.

FURTHER IDEAS

- To keep more of the leather texture visible, cut out an image and iron it onto the center of the case, leaving some of the original leather visible around the edge.

- Use contrasting—or even neon—embroidery floss (thread) to add a pop of color.

- You could decorate both sides, or incorporate text, such as a name or inspirational quote, into your design.

8 Using a sharp needle (for leather), thick thread (I used silver embroidery floss, doubled over for strength), and a thimble to help push the needle through the leather, blanket stitch along one side (starting at the top), along the bottom, and up the other side. Keep the holes an even distance from each other and from the edge at all times and remove the bulldog clips as you go. Tie off the thread.

PACKING TAPE FLORAL JEWELRY HOOKS

Using a simple packing-tape transfer technique and plain drawer pulls, turn your favorite floral photographs into unique, customized jewelry hooks. Of course, you don't have to use them for jewelry—why not fix them to a length of wood to create a custom coat rack or garden tool hanger? They can also bring a personal touch to a furniture makeover project if used as drawer pulls, or they can even become pretty curtain tie backs!

1 Paint the tops of the knobs with white paint (to make your transfer colors more vibrant) and set aside to dry. Avoid getting paint on the sides and sand away any errant paint once dry.

You will need

- Flat wooden knobs (available from most hardware stores and eBay)
- White paint
- Laser printer, or laser/photocopy prints (from a local copy shop)
- Clear packing tape
- Waxed paper
- PVA glue
- Paintbrush
- Sandpaper
- Bone folder (or the back of a tea spoon)
- Scissors
- Pencil
- Bowl of warm water

2 Print laser copies of the photos you want to use (or get laser or photocopies made at a copy shop). Lay the laser copy out, image side up, and smooth a strip of packing tape over the selected area. Continue until the whole area you want to use is covered, laying out strips of tape parallel to each other and overlapping by at least ¼ in. (5 mm). (Thin tape will require more strips than wider tape to cover the image, but you can use either.)

3 Burnish the packing tape with a flat, rounded end of a bone folder or the back of a teaspoon to get rid of any air bubbles and make the ink stick to the tape.

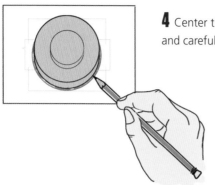

4 Center the knob face down over your image and carefully draw around it with a pencil.

5 Carefully cut along the pencil mark with scissors to cut out your disc.

Disposal

Dispose of the water by pouring it down the toilet rather than clogging your sink—or better still, recycle it into homemade paper.

6 Submerge the disc, tape side down, in a bowl of warm water and begin to rub the paper backing away with your thumb. Continue until the back of the tape feels smooth. Change the water for each disc, as it will fill with paper pulp.

FURTHER IDEAS

- Make all the designs the same for a matching set of hooks. Just get lots of laser prints or photocopies of the same photo.

- This project works with both black-and-white and color images.

- You can apply this technique to rounded or curved knobs, too, if you keep the design smaller and centered to avoid wrinkles.

7 Lay the disc on some waxed paper, shiny side down, and leave to dry. The stickiness will return once dry. If paper fiber is still visible, repeat step 6 again.

8 Apply a light coat of watered-down PVA glue to the sticky side of the disc and place it on the drawer knob. Press firmly and leave to dry. There's no need to seal it, as the tape does that for you!

- Select photos that complement the use to make staying organized a bit more fun—try puppy portraits for hanging dog leads, or kids' faces for their own coat and bag hooks.

WAX TRANSFER WOODEN PLATTER

Head to the kitchen and grab some waxed paper and a wooden serving platter, chopping board, or pizza paddle for this easy yet effective transfer project. Serve it up your way by freeing your favorite foodie photos from the small screen of Instagram and into a real culinary setting. Seal to keep it food safe for serving or style it up for some unique kitchen decoration. Apply to any wooden objects you like and print using classic black and white or get experimental with full color: the knocked-back results will be a knock out.

You will need

- Wooden board (untreated—no wax or varnish)
- Digital photo or scan of analog image
- US letter size (A4) office paper
- Double-sided tape
- Waxed paper
- Food-safe clear soft wax —I used Annie Sloan Soft Wax
- Tape measure
- Scissors
- Damp sponge or cloth
- Printer
- Old credit card
- Lint-free soft cloth

1 Measure the area of the board you wish to print onto.

2 Resize your image to these measurements. In image-editing software (see page 10), flip the image over into a mirror image (Image > Image Rotation > Flip Canvas Horizontal) as it will be reversed in the transfer; this is especially important if your image contains text. Darker images in black and white, ideally on a white background, work best, so convert your image to black and white on the computer if necessary (Image > Adjustments > Desaturate); alternatively, check the "Grayscale" box in your printer dialog box and the printer will convert it for you.

White background
For details of how to give your image a white background, see page 10.

3 Take one sheet of US letter size (A4) office paper and stick double-sided sticky tape along one short side close to the edge. Line this up with a straight edge of the waxed paper and press firmly (waxed paper has wax on both sides). Carefully trim the waxed paper down to the same size as the office paper on the remaining three sides. The supporting paper will help to feed the wax paper through the printer correctly. Make sure that the waxed paper is not creased, as this will affect the print quality.

4 Using a slightly damp sponge or cloth, lightly wipe over the wooden board to prime the receiving area. This will help the ink transfer. Take care, though, as too much dampness may make the ink run.

Trial and error

Experiment on scraps of wood or on the back of the board first to find the settings that work for you and your image. For paler results, apply your transfer to dry wood.

5 Feed the waxed paper into the printer, taped edge first and wax side up. Use a plain paper setting to avoid too much ink being deposited. Print your image and carefully guide the paper out.

6 Carefully peel away the office paper. Turn the wax paper ink side down, line it up over the board, and place it down in one decisive moment. No moving it or it will smudge!

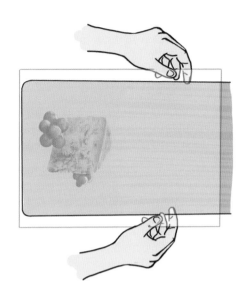

FURTHER IDEAS

- Any untreated wood should receive the ink well. Embellish crates, boxes, frames, stands, furniture, or a set of wooden blocks.

- Mix photos and text together to build your design or use colorful vintage fruit-crate labels as inspiration.

- This technique also works on fabric and (minus step 4) on painted metal.

7 Holding it very still, gently scrape an old credit card over the surface of the image to transfer the ink.

8 Gently remove the paper. Some ink will remain, so be careful. Leave to dry.

9 Using a lint-free soft cloth, seal with a clear soft wax that will be food safe when completely cured.

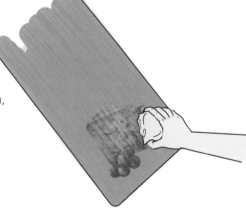

STATEMENT PHOTO DRAWERS

With a bit of elbow grease you can turn a basic, cheap, "nothing special" chest of drawers into a statement piece that would take pride of place in any decorating scheme. This project shows you how to take one special photograph, colorize it, enlarge it, tile it, and transfer it onto the furniture front. One step beyond simple découpage, this technique uses a gel medium for image transfer to encapsulate the ink from your laser prints. Rub the paper away to leave the ink behind, allowing the texture of the wood to remain visible and creating an ethereal and beautiful effect. Let any mistakes create a rustic look as the image itself does the talking.

You will need

- Chest of drawers
- Wood filler
- Multi-purpose decorative paint—I used Annie Sloan Chalk Paint™ in "Antoinette," which doesn't need a primer and creates a great base
- Digital photo or scan of analog image
- Découpage glue—I used Annie Sloan Découpage Glue and Varnish
- Clear soft wax
- Tape measure
- Medium-grit sandpaper
- 1-in. (2.5-cm) brush
- Craft knife, metal rule, and cutting mat
- Clean, lint-free cloths
- Pin

Optional (see step 6)

- Laser or inkjet printer
- Photo paper
- Flashdrive
- Damp sponge or cloth

1 Assemble the drawers minus the drawer knobs. Measure the area you want to cover. I measured the drawer fronts (excluding the top and sides of the carcass of the drawer unit) and also the front panel under the drawers. This is the minimum size for your sectional image if you want to cover the drawers completely.

2 Fill any holes (but not the drawer handle holes!) with wood filler. Leave to dry, then sand flat.

3 Paint the drawers in your chosen color. Paint the drawer knobs, too, and set aside. Apply a second coat if necessary and leave to dry again.

4 Scan your original photo into your computer (if it is not already there as a digital file).

- In image-editing software (see page 10), flip the image over into a mirror image (Image > Image Rotation > Flip Canvas Horizontal).
- First, I converted my image to black and white (Image > Adjustments > Desaturate) and increased the contrast (Image > Adjustments > Brightness/Contrast).

- To change the colors, go to "Variations" (Image > Adjustments >Variations)—I opted for "more magenta"—or play around with the hue and saturation options (Image > Adjustments > Hue/Saturation—or "Tint" for online editors).
- Enlarge (if needed) and crop to the drawer measurement from step 1 to give your image the correct ratio.

5 Choose an online image-tiling site (see page 143). Upload your image. Select how many "tiles" you would like and on what paper size. I chose US letter size (A4) paper, landscape and two sheets wide, because two pages of US letter size (A4) landscape is slightly more than the width I required. See what works for you within the preview features. Save the results by downloading the tiles.

6 If you have a laser printer, print out the PDF (using borderless printing to keep the size consistent) to produce one laser copy of each sheet. Print more if you want to do a test run first. Otherwise, email or flashdrive the PDF to a copy shop (or print the PDF out using an inkjet printer onto photo paper at high quality) and get a laser copy made of each sheet.

Create a pencil guide

If trimming the borders off means the image has shrunk, measure and drawer a faint pencil line down the center of the drawers and use this line as a guide when applying the paper sections.

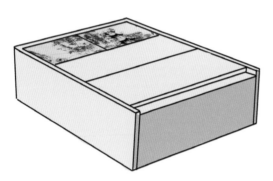

7 Using a craft knife and metal rule on a cutting mat, trim the white borders off your laser copies. Lay the chest of drawers flat on its back with the drawers in place, then lay the tiled laser copies out over the drawer fronts to check that they'll fit. Mark and make a small cut where the drawer edges are.

8 Paint a thin layer of découpage glue over the top drawer front and part way onto the second drawer down. Apply a thin, even layer of découpage glue to the image side of the top right page of your image. Apply the paper, image side down, to the left-hand side of the top drawer, aligning the top paper edge with the top of the drawer and the right side with the central pencil mark on the drawers (if you have one), and allowing the bottom edge to travel onto the next drawer (allow any space at the side if the image has shrunk). Smooth gently with a clean cloth to eliminate any air bubbles. Use a pin to prick any large air bubbles.

9 Repeat, sticking the top left page of your image to the right-hand side of the top drawer. Align the paper with the straight edge of the drawer top and the edge of the other paper.

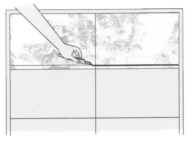

10 Very gently, using a sharp craft knife, cut along the gap between the top and middle drawer. Use a gentle sawing motion to avoid tearing the paper. Then push these edges of paper down flat around the drawer edges. Remove the middle drawer if it helps with access.

11 Repeat steps 8–10 on the remaining drawers and the front section under the drawers.

12 Using your fingers, wet the paper slightly and begin to rub in a circular motion, so that the paper starts to come away. Use a sponge or cloth instead if you prefer. Work away the first layer of paper. Continue wetting and rubbing until the image is clear, taking extra care around the edges. When dry, the image will look a little dull.

13 Once dried, apply clear soft wax all over the image with a clean cloth to make that last layer of paper fibers translucent and bring the image to life. Wax the knobs, too, and attach them to the drawers with the screws provided.

FURTHER IDEAS

- Paint the drawers in a pale color, as dark paint will obscure the transfer.

- Instead of covering the whole front, cut shapes out of the laser copies to apply in certain areas. Use this method to apply a small design to the center of a chair back, for example.

- For a bolder look, use a full-color image for the transfer.

FAMILY TABLE RUNNER

Bring a family focus to generic white table linen with this quick image-transfer project, which uses black-and-white photocopies, a natural cleaning product called Citra Solv, and an old teaspoon. Have a rummage through the archives and pick out full-length photos of people, then line them up on a fancy table runner to create new scenes. Celebrate a life by selecting pictures of a loved one from babyhood to old age, or use individual photos on a napkins as a novel way to set places at a dinner.

You will need
- Photos of people, preferably full length, or copies (see page 9)
- Plain white office paper
- Paper glue or repositionable spray adhesive
- Dry toner laser photocopies of your photos in black and white
- Plain white (or pale) cotton table runner, or other natural, flat-weave fabric
- Citra Solv concentrate
- Scissors
- Sticky tape
- Sheet of glass (or other flat, smooth, hard surface)
- Small pot
- Brush
- Bone folder or old teaspoon
- Iron
- Old towel

1 Cut around the edges of the people in your photographs—full-length photos (from head to toe) work best. Use copies if you don't want to cut up original photos or they need resizing.

2 Using glue, stick the people down on plain white office paper, lining them up in rows with a space between each one. At a copy shop that uses a dry toner laser copier, photocopy each sheet of paper in reverse/mirror image in black and white. For best results, use high-contrast copies. If the copies are light, ask the copy shop to darken them one or two stops on their machine.

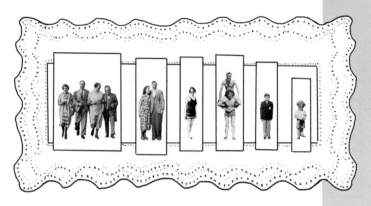

3 Lay the fabric out flat. Cut the paper to separate each person or group of people and decide where to place each one on the fabric. (Lining up the feet to just above the bottom edge creates a neat effect.)

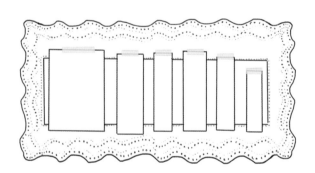

4 Once you are happy with the layout, turn the papers over so that they're image side down and stick a piece of sticky tape over the top edge of the paper to hold them in position.

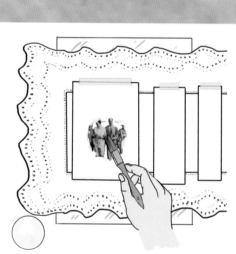

5 Place the glass on a clean work surface, then lay the fabric flat over the top, paper side up, with the left-hand image centered over the glass. Pour a small amount of Citra Solv into a pot. Dip the brush in, then lightly brush over the back of the paper, starting in the middle. The paper will become semi-transparent and you only need to "paint" where your image is.

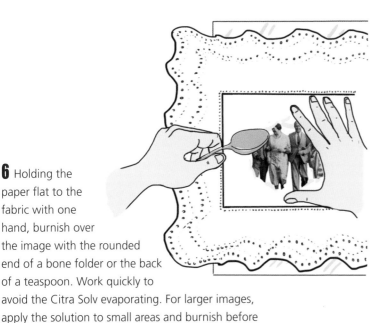

6 Holding the paper flat to the fabric with one hand, burnish over the image with the rounded end of a bone folder or the back of a teaspoon. Work quickly to avoid the Citra Solv evaporating. For larger images, apply the solution to small areas and burnish before moving on to the next area.

Checking your progress

You can lift the paper to see the results, but if you need to burnish more be sure to lay it back down in exactly the same position to avoid blurring the image.

7 Once the first image has been transferred, remove the sticky tape and used paper from the fabric. Move the fabric along to the left and align the next taped paper over the glass base. Working from left to right, repeat the process until all the images have been transferred. Leave to dry.

8 Press the fabric (on medium heat with no steam) in a well-ventilated area to fix the print. Protect the ironing board with an old towel. It can now be washed as normal.

Citra Solv

This product is available on Amazon, eBay, and from www.citrasolv.com.

FURTHER IDEAS

- Use photographs from different times in one person's life to create a personalized potted history. Or create family trees—just remember to leave room for new additions!

- This technique also works with color images (as long as they're toner-based laser copies—inkjets won't work).

- Instead of people, experiment with images of flowers, buildings, cars, or even more abstract imagery such as wrought-iron gates or other architectural decoration.

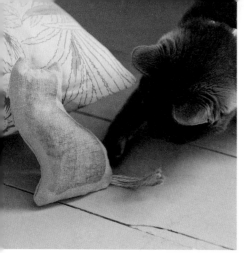

CATNIP TOY

Transferring your photographs onto fabric opens up a world of possibilities. Once the fabric has received the image, you can make anything with it. This catnip toy project starts with a laser copy of a pet photo heat transferred onto cotton. Sew a seam following the contour of your image and fill with stuffing, adding some catnip and a short string tail as a safe, playful element for some feline fun. Swap the catnip for lavender to make a sweet scented bag (for humans) or scale it up to make a one-of-a-kind pillow (cushion).

You will need

- Digital or analog photo of a cat, preferably sitting
- Two sheets plain white US letter size (A4) office paper
- Two pieces of cotton or linen (small weave for best results), 1½ in. (4 cm) larger all around than your image
- Wool or natural material scraps for stuffing
- 1 tablespoon catnip
- Four 4-in. (10-cm) lengths of natural twine
- Scissors
- Sheet of glass
- Sticky tape
- Wood-burning tool with pattern transfer head
- Old towel
- Pencil
- Pins
- Sewing thread
- Needle

Optional

- Iron

1 Cut around the cat in the photo (or resize (see page 12), print it out, and then cut it out) and stick it down on a sheet of plain white paper. I used an image 5 in. (12.5 cm) tall. Get a laser toner copy made of this, with the image flipped into "mirror" or "reverse." Inkjet prints won't work.

2 Place the sheet of glass on a clean work surface. Stretch out one piece of fabric and tape down each edge with sticky tape to keep it taut. (Iron first, if required.)

3 Center the laser copy cat image right side up on the fabric to check that it will fit inside the taped area. Then flip the image over and tape the top edge down to anchor it in position.

4 Fix the pattern transfer head (a wide, flat, disc shape) onto the wood burner tool and switch it on. Place the other sheet of white paper over the top of your taped image—this is to absorb some of the heat from the tool and to prevent your image paper from burning or scorching.

No image coming through?
You may just have a copy that won't work —it's the luck of the draw. Try again with a copy from another machine or shop.

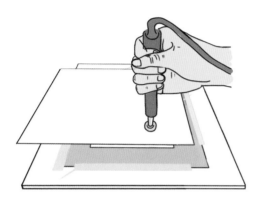

5 When the tool has heated up, wipe the end round and round on an old towel to take away a bit of the heat, then bring it down onto the paper (starting at the base of your image), keeping it constantly moving in a circular motion with the head flat to the paper and pressing quite hard.

6 Do this for about 20 seconds, then gently lift the safety paper and image paper up slightly to see how the transfer is progressing. If it's faint, press harder and for longer. If it's strong, move on to the next section above, keeping the paper you've worked on curled away from the fabric (to avoid ink going back onto the paper from the fabric).

7 Once the transfer is complete, lift and remove the paper. Using a pencil, draw a line 1 in. (2.5 cm) out from the edge of the cat transfer. You don't have to follow every contour, but keep to the basic outline of a cat. Then remove the tape and glass from the fabric.

8 Using sharp scissors, cut along the pencil line.

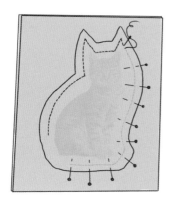

9 Take the second piece of fabric and lay it flat. Turn the cut-out fabric over, cat side down, and center it over the flat fabric, then pin the two layers together. Starting near the cat's tail, stitch the two pieces of fabric together using a backstitch and stitching about ¼ in. (5 mm) from the edge of the printed fabric. Leave a gap of about 2 in. (5 cm) at the base where the tail would be, and do not snip off the excess thread, as you'll need it to close up the gap later.

10 Trim away the excess from the bottom piece of fabric, then turn the whole thing right side out. Stuff with wool or material scraps (don't use polystyrene balls or anything that can be dangerous to cats if swallowed). Mix in one tablespoon of catnip.

11 Take four 4-in. (10-cm) lengths of twine and knot them together at one end. Stuff the knot inside the cat. Whipstitch the gap closed, using the thread left over from backstitching around the outline. Trim the tail down to 2 in. (5 cm) or shorter for safety.

FURTHER IDEAS

- The Citra Solv method (from the Family Table Runner on page 108) and the transfer artist paper method (from the Transfer Tote Bag on page 84) will also work.

Chapter 4
Using Light

In photography, light is everything—so be adventurous and explore new and unusual ways of using it in your photo art. From harnessing the power of sunlight to print on fabric to allowing light to shine through your images and transform them in ways that you could never imagine, this chapter brings us back to the original meaning of the word photography—"drawing with light."

VELLUM TEALIGHTS

Transform plain glass tealight holders into a beautiful personalized centerpiece by using printed vellum to create an etched-glass effect. Dig out your photos of impressive architecture and buildings—the castles, forts, temples, and cathedrals we encounter on our travels—or special locations much closer to home. Cut out windows to let the light twinkle through.

You will need

- Glass tealight holders, preferably with straight sides
- Digital photos or scans of analog images
- Thin vellum paper (80 gsm is good)
- Tape measure
- Inkjet or laser printer
- Scissors
- Repositionable spray adhesive
- Tealight candle

Optional

- Craft knife and cutting mat (if cutting out windows and rooftops)
- Clear all-purpose glue or double-sided tape

1 Measure around the outside of your tealight holder glass and note the circumference.

2 Prepare your digital photograph for printing (see page 10). Make sure that the width of the photograph is the same or slightly larger than the circumference of the glass. If it is not, scale it up under the "Resize" or "Image Size" tab.

3 As vellum is non-absorbent, the ink will just sit on the surface, so in your printer dialog box select "Print Quality" as "Economy," "Draft," or "Fast" to avoid a surplus of ink being deposited.
- Select the "Media Type" as "Transparency." If your printer doesn't have that setting, set it to "Plain Paper" instead.
- Under the "Color" options, select "Grayscale," so that the printer produces a black-and-white print rather than color.
- Feed a sheet of vellum into your inkjet printer. If the printer doesn't "take" it, place a piece of plain paper underneath it so that the printer can grab it more easily.
- Print your image and carefully remove the vellum from the printer tray. Set the print aside for at least 20 minutes, so that the ink can dry.

4 Once dry, trim your images with the scissors. The ink may still smudge, so handle the print carefully.

5 Using small, sharp scissors or a craft knife on a cutting mat, carefully cut around the rooftops of your vellum image. (You can skip this step if you'd like all of the glass to remain "frosted" by the vellum.)

Careful cutting
Use a craft knife and cutting mat to cut out some of the windows in the buildings, creating holes for the light to shine through.

FURTHER IDEAS

- Use colored copies for a more vibrant effect—or a different subject matter entirely!

- Scale up to decorate larger candle holders such as flat-sided storm lanterns.

- Convert three or four small picture frames into a tealight surround by removing the backs, cutting and gluing your vellum prints into the frames, and using a glue gun to fix the frames together along the long sides.

6 Lightly spray the back of the vellum with spray adhesive and carefully wrap it around your glass. If you left a slight excess on your print, use this overlap to stick the vellum edges together.

7 Line up the straight edge at the bottom of the print with the bottom edge of your tealight glass or, if the image is taller than your glass, line up the part of the image you like and trim away any excess. Let dry.

8 Insert a tealight candle to light or use an electronic one instead.

Reinforcing the seam
Use all-purpose glue or a strip of double-sided tape along the seam for added strength.

PINPRICK LANDSCAPE LAMPSHADE

This project shows you how to turn a plain (hum) drum lampshade into a panoramic vista, using a landscape photograph from your travels. A snowy mountain range by day, at night when the lamp is lit, the stars come out to play. Create your own constellations and highlights, using simple pinpricks to bring your image alive after dark.

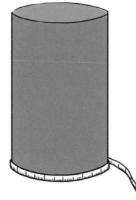

1 Measure the circumference of the lampshade. Your photograph will need to be printed to this width, so that it can wrap all the way round.

2 Select a landscape photograph of a mountain view or a city skyline that has a fairly even horizon line. Disregard the sky in the photo, as this will be cut away. Resize the photo (see page 12) so that the width of the image is the same (or greater) than the circumference of your lampshade. Don't worry about the height at this point, as this can be adjusted later. Make any other image adjustments such as saturation, contrast, or color on the computer if required (see pages 11–12).

3 To print the image, upload your photo to an online printer who print custom panoramas and order a print on self-adhesive vinyl to fit your lampshade. Alternatively, on your computer, print out your resized photo on a roll of inkjet printer paper to create one continuous print.

You will need
- Drum- or cylinder-shaped lampshade in a pale color
- Digital photo of a landscape
- Self-adhesive vinyl print (available from photo stores and printing companies—see page 142)
- Lamp base
- Tape measure
- Scissors
- Pin

Optional
- Roll of inkjet printer paper
- Inkjet printer
- Craft knife
- Repositionable spray adhesive

4 Using scissors, carefully cut away the sky part of your print, cutting along the horizon line of your image.

5 Wrap the image around the shade and check the height of the horizon line. If it's too high, move the print down the shade to expose more "sky" area for the pinpricks.

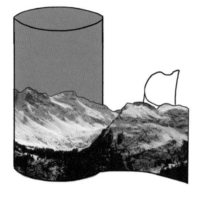

6 For self-adhesive vinyl prints, remove the backing paper from the left-hand edge. Align the left-hand edge of the print with the seam of the lampshade and the bottom edge of the print with the bottom edge of the lampshade. Carefully smooth the print onto the shade, working from left to right and peeling away the backing paper as you go. The edges should align, but if there is any excess, trim it away with a craft knife before sticking down.

Ready-made lampshades

If you are using a ready-made lampshade instead of a lampshade kit, wrap the print around the shade and trim the horizons to align with each other at the point where the two edges meet. This will help to make the image look continuous once it is fixed in place. If there's a seam in the shade, align the print seam with it also.

7 For prints made on an inkjet printer roll, apply repositionable spray adhesive to the back of the print and carefully wrap it around the shade, smoothing out any wrinkles as you go.

8 Fix the shade onto a lamp base and turn on the light. Taking care to protect your hands from the bare bulb, which will get hot, use a pin to prick holes through the shade, densely along the horizon and becoming more sparse as you reach the top of the shade. Continue until you are happy with the results.

FURTHER IDEAS

- Use star maps for inspiration if you want to trace actual constellations into the "sky."

- Avoid sunny daytime photos, as they jar visually with the stars in the sky (night). Opt instead for shots taken at dusk or play with the colors and saturation to give your sunny photo a more subdued look.

- Cityscapes, fireworks, photos taken at night, illuminated signage, or even portraits would work. Stick the entire image across the whole shade, including the sky, and use the pinpricks to highlight or frame areas of your image.

Let there be light!
Use pins of varying thickness for larger and smaller holes (larger holes will let more light through).

PICTURE FRAME LIGHT BOX

Using back lighting to make an image stand out is usually reserved for movie posters at the cinema or huge advertising boxes at bus stops or as billboards. This project explains how to create your own stunning light box for the home, using a decorative picture frame, some cut wood and Perspex, an LED light kit (available from the high street), your printer, and some backlit film (just make sure you buy the right kind for your printer—laser or inkjet). Turn your photography into gallery-quality art and create a focal (and talking) point for any room.

You will need

- Sturdy picture frame (any size that accommodates the LED strips)
- Clear Perspex or acrylic sheet, ⅛ in. (2 or 3 mm) thick
- Opal Perspex or acrylic sheet, ⅛ in. (2 or 3 mm) thick
- MDF, ½ in. (12 mm) and ¼ in. (6 mm) thick (see steps 2–4)
- Ten 1-in. (25-mm) wood screws
- Glue gun, wood glue, or all-purpose glue
- LED light kit
- Backlit film to suit your printer
- Digital photo or scan of analog image
- Tape measure
- Pencil
- Drill
- Junior hacksaw
- Screwdriver, or screwdriver bit for the drill
- Inkjet or laser printer
- Craft knife, metal rule, and cutting mat

Optional

- Sandpaper
- Electrical tape
- Hooks and fixings for hanging
- Wood filler
- Paint and paintbrush

1 Measure the frame, outer edge to outer edge from top to bottom and side to side. Make a note of these measurements. Remove the back panel of the frame, any paper inside, and the glass or Perspex, leaving you with just the frame. Also remove any plates or fixings that may be attached. Measure the inside edge of the frame (including the rebate "lip" where the

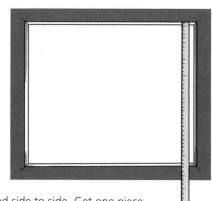

glass would sit) from top to bottom and side to side. Get one piece of clear and one piece of opaque acrylic sheet cut to these measurements. Check that both acrylic panels fit in the rebate (if they are slightly out, sand the edges of the rebate until they fit).

2 Cut two pieces of ½-in. (12-mm) -thick MDF to 3½ in. (90 mm) x the height of the frame minus ⅜ in. (10 mm). This allows the frame to have a ¼-in. (5-mm) "lip" on all sides for aesthetics (and also builds in some contingency space!).

3 Subtract 1⅜ in. (34 mm) from the width of the frame measurement. This 1⅜ in. (34 mm) is made up of 2 x ¼-in. (5-mm) allowances for the "lip" around the edge of the frame and also 2 x ½-in. (12-mm) allowances for where the ½-in. (12-mm)-thick MDF side panels from step 2 will be positioned. Cut two pieces of ½-in. (12-mm)-thick MDF to 3½ in. (90 mm) x your final figure reached above. That's the tricky part—cutting the sides of the box—done!

4 From ¼-in. (6-mm) MDF, cut a piece for the back of the box measuring the height of your frame minus ⅜ in. (10 mm) x the width of your frame minus ⅜ in. (10 mm). Now mark a ½-in. (12-mm) border along each edge in pencil to allow for fixing the sides of the box. In the center of this ½-in. (12-mm) border, mark in pencil a cross 1½ in. (40 mm) from each corner on all four sides. Mark also the center point of the two long sides. On a workbench or protected area, drill pilot holes through the MDF at these ten points.

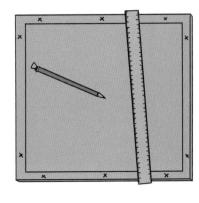

5 On a workbench or protected area, drill pilot holes through the MDF at the ten points marked with a cross.

6 Check your progress by placing the frame face down and placing the wooden pieces into position. They should form a box that fits together.

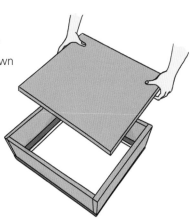

7 Taking the panel from step 3 that will be at the bottom of the frame, mark a ⅜-in. (1-cm) square in the top right corner. Using a junior hacksaw or similar, cut this square out to make a hole for the electrical cable.

Ready-made width gauge
The border is exactly the same width as the thickness of the MDF used for the box sides. To avoid fiddly measuring and marking, place a piece ½-in. (12-mm) MDF on its side on each edge in turn and draw along the other side in pencil.

8 To assemble the sides, take the two MDF pieces from step 2 and mark a ½-in. (12-mm) border along each short edge of both pieces. Make three marks within each border—one central and one at least ½ in. (12 mm) in from each corner. Drill pilot holes though these marks.

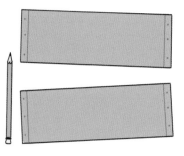

9 Using a screwdriver (or a drill with a screwdriver bit), screw a wood screw through each hole—far enough for the screw to stay in the hole, but not enough to appear through the other side.

10 Apply hot glue, wood glue, or all-purpose glue to the ends of the side panels and line up all the sides. Screw the wood screws home to create your box. Leave to dry.

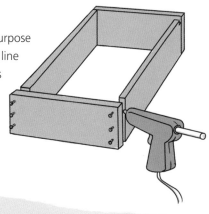

11 Position the box on the frame back (ensure the side of the box with the hole for the cable is not touching the frame) to check that it fits. Apply hot glue, wood glue, or all-purpose glue to the edges of the box and press firmly onto the back of the frame. Leave to dry.

Different LED arrangements

For larger frames, you may wish to wire the LED strips differently—see the manufacturer's instructions for possible permutations.

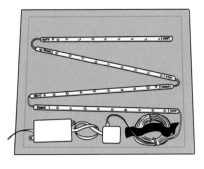

Cable tidies

If you have a lot of excess cables, keep them tidy and fix into place with electrical tape.

12 To assemble the LED kit, clip four LED strips together in a line and connect to the junction box. Lay everything out on the back of the box, so that it all fits within the border lines drawn in step 4 and the cable extends out at the bottom right corner (to align with the hole cut in step 7 for the cable). Once you are happy with your layout, begin to fix the elements in place, using the adhesive pads and other fixings that come with the LED kit.

13 To print your photograph, refer to the measurement you took inside the frame rebate in step 1—this is the minimum size for printing your image, so resize your image to fit (see page 12). Print your image on the rough side of the backlit film, and leave to dry. Alternatively, you can order prints up to any size in backlit film or duratrans film for lightboxes from print shops, signmakers, and online printers.

14 Trim your image to size by placing one of the acrylic panels over the artwork and cutting carefully around the edge with a sharp craft knife and metal rule on a cutting mat.

15 Remove the protective plastic from the clear acrylic panel. Apply all-purpose glue carefully inside the rebate of the frame, taking care not to go over the edge onto the visible part of the frame, and gently place the acrylic panel in position. Leave to dry.

16 Keeping the area dust free, insert the print into the frame rebate, image side down.

17 Now remove the protective plastic from the opaque acrylic panel and glue that in place on top of the print. Leave to dry.

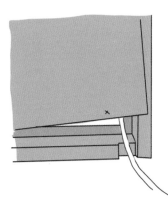

18 Take the back panel and turn it LED side down over the box, lining up the cable with the cable hole.

19 Place the back in position, aligning the edges. Use the screwdriver (or drill and screwdriver bit) to screw in the woodscrews in all the pre-drilled pilot holes.

20 Check the box is working by flicking on the switch and then place as required. For wall hanging, attach suitable picture hooks or mirror plates to the back and use the correct wall fixings for your wall type. If you wish, fill, sand, and paint the exterior.

FURTHER IDEAS

- Adapt the box to have a slot on one side to slide in the photograph (sandwiched between the two sheets of acrylic) if you want to easily change the image on display.

- Use ready-made boxes, such as old wooden drawers or crates. Create a hole for the cable, fix the LEDs into the base, fit the acrylic sheets and photograph into the picture frame, and then glue the picture frame onto the box.

- Omit the photograph from the lightbox to create a blank, opaque, backlit picture frame. Experiment with hanging slides in front or printing photos onto self-adhesive clear sticker paper for temporary and changeable displays.

SUN PRINT NEGATIVE TIE

Once upon a time, taking photos involved not really knowing what you'd captured until the prints arrived back from the lab inside a paper envelope along with strips of developed film (that would usually always fall out). If you wanted a reprint, these negatives would be the source. Handled with care, they're good to print from again and again. Using a product called Inkodye, sunlight, and some of these negative strips, you can custom print a tie in your choice of color. No negs? That's ok. Just invert a photo and print it onto Inkofilm or clear acetate to create your own.

You will need

- Strip of negatives (or a digital photo and clear acetate sheet for inkjet printer)
- Clear adhesive tape
- White silk tie (or ribbon or scarf), or other natural, close-weave fiber such as fine cotton
- Inkodye photo printing kit (see page 142)
- Old towel
- Large board or tray
- Masking tape
- Paper towels
- Sheet of glass (non UV blocking)
- Sunlight
- Washing machine

Optional

- Inkjet printer

1 Decide on a strip of negatives to use. If you don't have any, you can create your own from a digital photo (see page 11), then print it at high quality on the matt side of the Inkofilm from the kit (or on acetate sheets for inkjet printers). For best results, print two copies and layer one over the other, perfectly aligned, to create an extra-dark negative. Tape them together with clear tape.

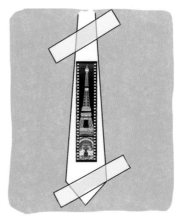

2 Lay an old towel out flat over a large board or tray. Lay the tie down flat, right side up, on top of the towel. Using masking tape, mask off the bottom section of the tie on the diagonal. Lay the negatives out where you'd like them to print on the tie to check that they fit. Mask off the tie with another strip of tape above the negs, also on the diagonal. Remove the negs and set them aside.

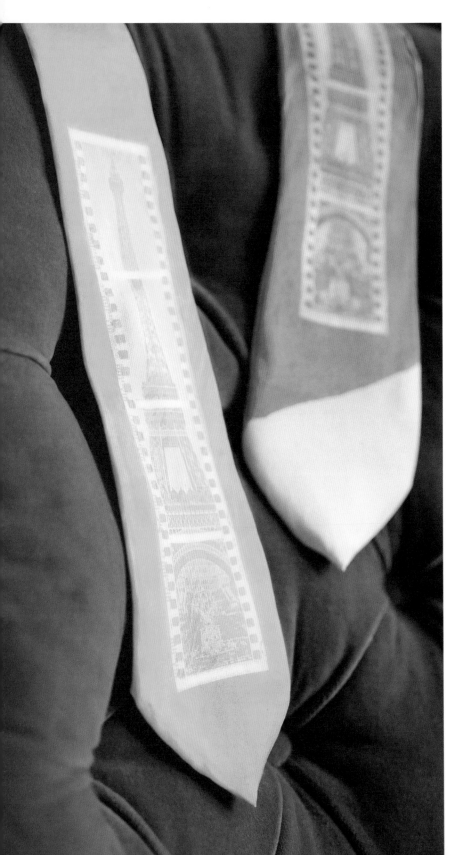

3 Working in a well-ventilated area in subdued light (any light will start the development process, so you have to work quite quickly), take your chosen color of Inkodye from the kit, shake it, snap it open by folding in half, and then spread the ink onto the tie inside the area masked by tape. The area should be damp; if it is too wet, blot with a paper towel to remove the excess ink.

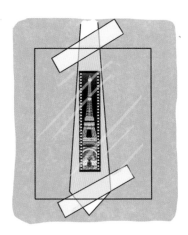

4 Place the negatives in position, shiny side down, then place a sheet of glass over the top to keep it all flat.

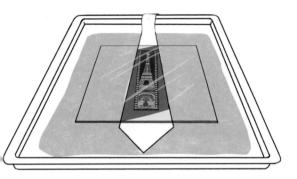

5 Pick up the tray and take it into an area of direct sunlight. Expose for 10–15 minutes on a sunny day or 20–30 minutes on a cloudy day. You will see the color develop, but leave it exposed for the allotted time to help the color "fix."

Shiny side down

The rough side of the acetate is the side the negative has been "printed" onto. Contact between the chemicals and the rough side could degrade the negative image, whereas with the smooth, shiny side, the negative image is protected.

Getting a sharp print

This process can be done indoors—you don't have to take the tray outside. I exposed my image indoors using the direct sunlight coming in through my glass window. However, if you do take the tray outside, make sure that the negs are secured so that they won't move in a breeze, as any movement will blur the image.

6 Once exposed, remove the negatives from the tie. Wipe the negatives clean on the waterproof (shiny) side with a damp paper towel and store flat for future use. Remove the masking tape from the tie.

7 Machine wash the tie twice using the Inkowash detergent from the kit, on a hot wash and a cold rinse cycle. Once this step is complete, your Inkodye prints are permanent and can be worn and washed normally.

FURTHER IDEAS

- A tie works as it's long and thin, but you could try this with ribbons, too. For enlarged negatives and single images, experiment with scarves and T-shirts (place a board inside to avoid printing onto the back, too)—in fact, anything that is made with a natural fiber.

- Use it to print onto fabric, then cut and sew your own creations—pillows (cushions), napkins, zip bags, and so on.

- Apply the ink with splashes or rollers, or expose the whole tie to give it a completely new color.

CYANOTYPE PURSE

Using cotton pre-treated with cyanotype chemicals, it's very easy to print your own designs with just a negative and sunlight. The fabric can then be made into small bags and purses, or used in patchwork or other sewing projects. For this sweet little purse, I used a negative of tailor's dummies to print a photo-realistic image for one side; for the other side, I simply placed sewing-related objects over the fabric before exposing it to the sun to create a photogram. Cyanotype printing produces lovely blue and cyan tones against white and is a simple yet magical process that kids will love, too.

You will need

- Negative or digital photo
- US letter size (A4) clear acetate sheet for inkjet printers
- Two 8½-in. (21.5-cm) pre-treated white cotton squares (available from www.blueprintsonfabric.com)
- Objects for photogram (scissors, pins, thread, bobbins etc.)
- 8-in. (20-cm) zipper
- Thread
- Scanner
- Printer
- Tray
- Sheet of glass (non UV blocking)
- Pins
- Scissors
- Zipper foot for sewing machine
- Sewing machine
- Pinking shears

Optional

- Sheet of card stock (card)
- Paper towel

1 To create a large negative, scan in your original negative (landscape orientation works best) and save the file. Alternatively, open your digital photo, convert to black-and-white (Image > Adjustments > Desaturate), increase the contrast (Image > Adjustments > Brightness/Contrast) and convert to a negative (Image > Adjustments >Invert). Scale your file up to 7½ in. (19 cm) wide and print out on the acetate sheet, using standard settings. Make sure to print onto the coated "rough" side. Let dry.

2 In an area out of direct sunlight, open the bag of pre-treated fabric squares and take out one sheet, making sure to seal the bag again to protect the remaining fabric. Lay the sheet out flat on a tray or similar portable flat surface. For stability, you can pin it by the corners to a sheet of card stock (just be aware that pins may cast shadows that will also print).

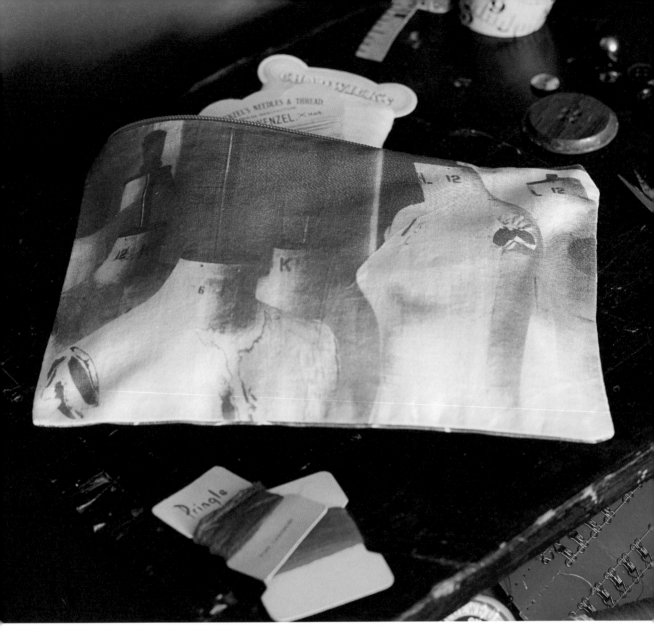

3 Lay the negative shiny side down over the fabric, then lay a sheet of glass over the top to keep the negative pressed firmly against the fabric for a sharp print.

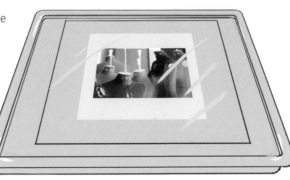

4 Place the tray in direct sunlight. Leave for 5–10 minutes on a sunny day or 15–30 minutes on a cloudy day to expose the fabric.

5 Once exposed, remove the tray from direct sunlight. Remove the negative (wipe it clean with a damp paper towel if you wish to reuse it) and rinse the fabric thoroughly in clean, cold water until the water runs clear. Lay flat, out of direct sunlight, until dry.

6 To create a photogram, lay out a square of pre-treated fabric, as in step 2, then place your selected objects on the fabric; I used sewing scissors, bobbins, safety pins, pins, a thimble, and some embroidery floss (thread) to create my design. Then expose the fabric, following steps 4 and 5.

7 Press the fabric with a dry iron. (The blue color will change slightly when warm but will return to the original color when cool.)

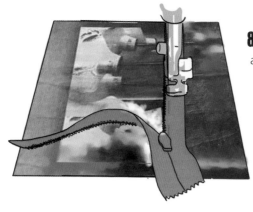

8 Place the zipper and one piece of fabric right sides together, aligning the zipper with the top edge of your printed photo. Pin in place. Fit a zipper foot to your sewing machine, then machine stitch along the edge of the zip. Cut away the excess fabric behind the zipper tape with pinking shears.

9 Repeat for the second piece of fabric, lining it up with the first.

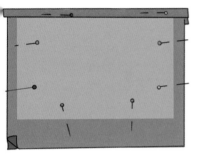

10 Open the zip so that you will be able to turn the bag right side out later. Pin the two sides right sides together around the edge of the printed photo, carefully aligning the edges. Change back to a normal sewing machine foot and machine stitch around the sides and base of the printed photo.

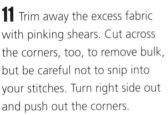

11 Trim away the excess fabric with pinking shears. Cut across the corners, too, to remove bulk, but be careful not to snip into your stitches. Turn right side out and push out the corners.

FURTHER IDEAS

- Use photographic prints on both sides, or make the back of the bag out of another complementary fabric.

- You can use almost anything to create a photogram (as long as it's dry). Select things that complement the theme of your photographs. Objects from nature such as ferns, feathers, and leaves work well. Alternatively, make your own—for example, if you print a winter snap of kids playing in the snow, they could make paper-cut snowflakes to use for the photogram. Or you could use cut-out letters to spell out words and names.

"STAINED-GLASS" WINDOW

Make your own colorful "stained-glass" window decorations using vintage transparencies (slides). Look for slide collections in forgotten corners of the attic, on auction sites, or at vintage fairs, or turn your digital images into transparencies by printing them on clear acetate. By cutting and taping clear plastic sleeves (designed for archiving film media) together, you can create displays in any shape or size you desire. Suction-cup clips are a simple way to hang your creation in a light-soaked window—then let the sun reveal the true beauty of this almost forgotten process.

You will need

- At least 37 x 35-mm slides
- Clear adhesive tape, 1 in. (25 mm) wide
- Three sheets of clear negative storage sheets for 35-mm film (each one has two sections with five columns per section)
- Card stock (card)
- Colored gels for photography or colored acetate or cellophane (from craft shops)
- Four clear suction cups with clip attachment
- Small flathead screwdriver
- Scissors
- Bone folder
- Craft knife, metal rule, and cutting mat
- White cotton glove

1 Remove the slides from their mounts (you may need to use a small flat-head screwdriver to prise the mounts apart). Group them in nine sets of four (setting aside the last single slide), arranging them by subject or color, as you wish.

2 Align four slides in a vertical column, placing the shiny side of the slide—the front—face down (the back has a matt appearance). Cut a piece of clear adhesive tape about 1½ in. (4 cm) in length and carefully tape the bottom of one slide to the top of the next, carefully aligning the side edges and leaving no gap in between. Repeat until you have a column of four slides, then trim away the excess tape with scissors. Run a bone folder over the tape to get a good seal and eliminate any air bubbles.

3 Repeat step 2 to create nine separate columns with four slides in each.

4 Take one clear negative sheet and place it face down on a clean surface (the back will be one smooth surface and the front has the channels the film slides into). Now place another sheet, also face down, above the first sleeve, lining up the sides, with the top sheet overlapping the bottom sheet by ⅛–¼ in. (3–5 mm) or so. Tape across this join to create one long sleeve, then run a bone folder over the tape to eliminate any air bubbles. Trim the excess tape from the two sides.

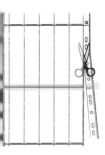

5 Using scissors, carefully trim away the border where holes are punched for ringbinders, cutting outside the little dots that form the seal for the edge of the outer channel. Also cut away the excess from the other side, leaving just the five vertical channels with all their seals intact.

6 Each "channel" is designed to house a strip of film that is 1⅜ x 6 in. (35 x 150 mm), so measure that out on a piece of thick card stock with a pencil and ruler. Using a sharp craft knife and metal rule on a cutting mat, carefully cut it out to create a template.

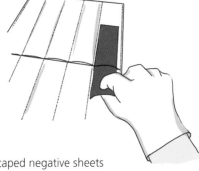

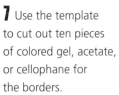

7 Use the template to cut out ten pieces of colored gel, acetate, or cellophane for the borders.

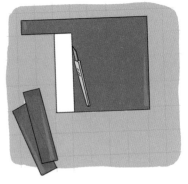

8 Turn the taped negative sheets over. Wearing a white cotton glove, wipe your fingers over the first piece of gel to remove any dust, then carefully slide the gel into the bottom left channel. Repeat for the bottom right channel and then continue filling the outer channels on all four sections to complete the sides of the colored frame.

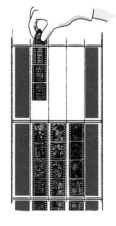

9 Insert your columns of slides from step 2 shiny side up. First, fill the two bottom sections. Hold it up to the light to check you have the slides where you want them; they can be removed and swapped about easily if not. For the next section up, cut an arch shape in the top slide of each outer column, to emphasize the stained-glass window design, and then insert as before.

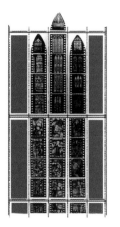

10 Take the reserved single slide and cut it into an arch shape. Insert it into the central channel of the top section and work it all the way down to the bottom of the channel.

11 To create the base of the frame, take the third negative sheet and cut out a single channel two sections high. Cut outside the seal "dots" so that the contents can stay in. Insert a piece of colored gel into each section.

12 Place the slide artwork face down and turn the new channel section right side down and at right angles to the bottom of the artwork, centering it over the middle column of slides. Overlap by ⅛–¼ in. (3–5 mm), tape in place, and run the bone folder over it. Using a craft knife and metal rule on a cutting mat, trim away the excess channel on both sides.

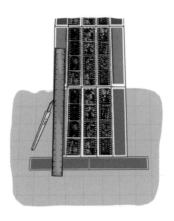

13 To create the top of the frame, cut another single channel two sections high—but this time leave an extra ⅝ in. (1.5 cm) on the right-hand side for fixing later. (This is essentially ⅝ in. (1.5 cm) of the neighboring channel.)

14 Cut a straight line across the artwork just above the top of the single arched slide, roughly 1¾ in. (4.5 cm) up from the join with the top of the third sleeve. Remove the two colored gels from the section you've just cut off and set them aside.

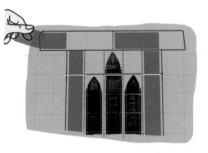

15 Take the section cut for the top of the frame and turn it at right angles to the top of the artwork, aligning the edge with the seal dots. Both pieces should be right side down. Overlap them slightly and tape together. Run the bone folder over the tape to remove any air bubbles. Re-insert the two colored gels you set aside earlier. Trim away the excess at each side to complete the frame.

16 Measure the empty pockets left on each side of the central arched slide and cut two pieces of a different-colored gel to this size. Insert to complete your "stained glass."

17 Take the suction cups with clip attachment and gently clip one onto each corner of the "stained glass." Use the suction cups to stick your artwork to window glass or another backlit surface.

FURTHER IDEAS

- Art supply stores sell multipacks of colored gels, so you can use lots of different colors. If you have trouble finding those, use cellophane candy wrappers cut to size instead.

- Keep the slides in their mounts for a retro look. Instead of negative sheets, use sleeves for mounted slides, which have individual pockets to tuck each slide into. Space them out and fill the remaining pockets with colored gels to create a patchwork effect.

- Adapt the project to fill any size of window by taping more sleeves together or trimming them as necessary. For round or curved windows, just tape and cut the sleeves to fit before you fill them with the photography.

- Instead of slides, use the negatives for which these sleeves were designed; they are already in strips, but they're darker, so go for graphic shapes.

- Display cinefilm. Although it's much smaller in size, you can display the narrative of the film at one glance.

TEMPLATES

These templates are for the "Watch the Birdie"
Mobile project (page 72). They are full-size templates,
so you can simply trace them off the page.

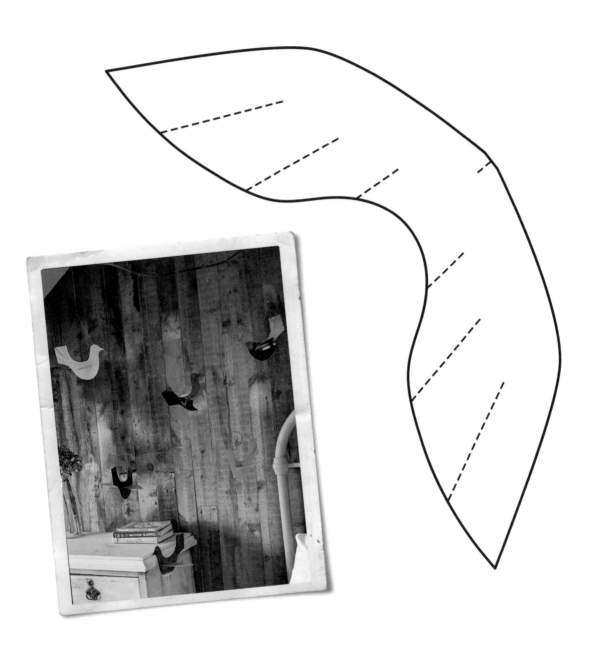

USEFUL RESOURCES

AUTHOR WEBSITES

Show me what you make!
www.facebook.com/EllieLaycockAuthor

ELLIE LAYCOCK PHOTOGRAPHY
www.ellielaycock.co.uk

HUNTED AND STUFFED
Luxury homeware made with upcycled
vintage textiles; ships worldwide.
www.huntedandstuffed.com
Twitter: @huntednstuffed

US SUPPLIERS

ANNIE SLOAN
Tel: 504-305-5531
www.anniesloanunfolded.com

BLUEPRINTS ON FABRIC
Hand-treated light-sensitive fabrics.
20504 81st Ave., SW, Vashon Island,
WA 98070
Tel: 206-463-3369; toll free: 800-631-3369
www.blueprintsonfabric.com

CITRA SOLV
Use their website to find a local or
online retailer near you.
Tel: 800-343-6588 or 203-778-0881
www.citrasolv.com

EZPRINTS
Online printing service for custom sizes
and panoramas.
Tel: 866-469-5356
www.ezprints.com

HOLLANDER'S
Specialists in bookbinding supplies and
decorative papers.
Tel: 734-741-7531
www.hollanders.com

LESLEY RILEY
Famous Transfer Artist Paper.
www.lesleyriley.com

LUMI (INKODYE)
Online store that ships internationally.
www.lumi.co

UK SUPPLIERS

FRED ALDOUS
Art and craft supplies.
37 Lever Street, Manchester M1 1LW
Tel: 0161 236 4224
www.fredaldous.co.uk

BUCH & BOX
Fine decorative papers.
www.etsy.com/uk/shop/buchundbox

CRAFTY ARTS
Online art and craft store including
foam boards.
Tel: 020 7993 5479
www.craftyarts.co.uk

CRAFTY COMPUTER PAPER
Online store for transfer and
decal papers.
Tel: 01162 744 755
www.craftycomputerpaper.co.uk

GLOBAL APE
Printer ink stockists.
Tel: 07823 762 077
www.globalape.com

JACKSON'S ART SUPPLIES
For paints, brushes, gesso, and varnishes;
stores in London and Gloucester, plus
online sales.
Tel: 0844 499 8430
www.jacksonsart.com

MY BIG POSTER
Online store for custom-sized
photo prints.
www.mybigposter.co.uk

PAPERCHASE
For paper, card, gift wrap, and much
more; stores nationwide and online.
www.paperchase.co.uk

PHOTOFUSION
Photography courses, plus scanning,
retouching, and printing services.
17A Electric Lane, London SW9 8LA
Tel: 020 7738 5774
www.photofusion.org

PURE DISPLAY
For backlit inkjet paper/film.
Tel: 01923 468 885
www.puredisplay.com

RYMAN
Nationwide stores offering color
photocopying.
Tel: 0800 801 901
www.ryman.co.uk

SHEPHERDS INC. FALKINER FINE PAPERS
Fine bookbinding materials supplier,
based in London.
Tel: 020 7233 9999
store.bookbinding.co.uk

SILVERPRINT
For photographic supplies.
120 London Road, London SE1 6LF
Tel: 020 7620 0169
www.silverprint.co.uk

ANNIE SLOAN
Chalk paint and waxes.
Tel: 01865 803 168
www.anniesloan.co.uk

UK CARD CRAFTS
For online craft supplies, including
acetate and vellum.
www.ukcardcrafts.com

THE VANILLA VALLEY
Baking supplies, including wax paper
and glycerin.
Tel: 0800 917 1419
www.thevanillavalley.co.uk

YOLO
Stockists of image transfer papers and
printable cotton canvas.
Tel: 020 8240 0658
www.yolo.co.uk

INDEX

ACKNOWLEDGMENTS

Thank you so much to CICO Books for allowing me to explore, play, and create. Special thanks go to Cindy Richards, Sally Powell, Penny Craig, the wonderful Carmel Edmonds who kept me on track, my lovely editor Sarah Hoggett and fine illustrator Harriet De Winton, designer Vicky Rankin, plus Stephen, Fahema, Gordana, and the CICO team. Thanks to stylist Joanna Thornhill and photographer James Gardiner who, despite me giving them some of the most technically difficult things to photograph, did a sterling job. Also to my family, friends, and everyone else who supported me in so many ways—I thank you.